12 msc

The First Dail

The First Dail

January 21st 1919

by

MAIRE COMERFORD

Published by
JOE CLARKE,
68 Upper O'Connell St.,
Dublin.

Cover Design
JOE COMERFORD.

976544

941.59   31/7/7C

Printed by Vanessa Press on Irish paper.

CONTENTS

APPENDICES

ILLUSTRATIONS

The first meeting.

Countess Markievicz home from prison.

The soldier's vote.

The Post Office and Nelson's Pillar in 1818.

Personalities 1916-'21.

Dáil Éireann, April 10th, 1919.

The Local Government Elections, 1920.

Protest outside Mountjoy Jail.

Limerick paper money.

Partition.

Burning British government out of the Custom House.

The first session of the first Dáil Éireann—Seats had been prepared for 105 members. Cathal Brugha is Ceann Comhairle and Count Plunkett is reading the Message to the Free Nations of the World.

INTRODUCTION

MOST of those to whom I owe a grateful acknowledgment for their part in this work are now dead. Some are national heroes, admired at a distance. I have drawn from their writings and their names are given. It is not fair that we who stand by the 1916 graves at commemoration times should sometimes do so without having taken the trouble to understand the message which the Proclamation of the Provisional Government of the Irish Republic was intended to convey to us. That plan was adopted by the first Dáil Éireann; but what happened to it? It is more than ever relevant to-day.

There were, and are, others to whom I am indebted for their wisdom, their courage, their great experience and their interest in the youth fifty years ago, when it was sheer joy to us to be alive and taking part in a fight for Ireland and justice, shoulder to shoulder with our own nation at ground level. In my memory such men and women were Rev. John Francis Sweetman, O.S.B., Alice Stopford Green, Gobnait ni Bruadair, Aine Ceannt, Sean Etchingham, Charlie Murphy, Hannah Sheehy Skeffington—all dead now. Then there were the families who accepted me into comradeship, the Woods, the Humphreys, the Plunketts, the Phelans, the O'Donnells, the Barrys. This was only one segment of the great chain of friendships which extended at home and abroad, wherever the Irish were in revolt. This book brings my greeting to all the friends who know they helped me, and to those who may never know it, particularly to those who are now, perhaps, very poor, as well as being very old. They gave what they had, when they had it.

CHAPTER 1

DÁIL ÉIREANN assembled for the first time in the Round Room of Dublin's Mansion House, on January 21st, 1919. Thirty, out of a possible 105 members answered the roll. Between them they represented thirty one constituencies because Eoin MacNeill had been successful both in Derry City and for the National University of Ireland. Thirty three republicans who would have been there if they could, were in prison, most of them without trial since the previous May 17th—this figure would have been 34 except that Pierce McCann, of Tipperary East, had died in jail. Neither the ending of the first World War —November 11th—nor the elections had brought any change in King George's prisons!

At the first meeting Leinster was represented by fourteen T.D.s, Munster by eight, and Ulster and Connacht by four each. Invitation to attend the Dáil were sent to all the 104 men, and one woman who were successful at the polls on December 14th, 1918. Of these 73 were republicans; most of them had fought in the Easter Rising, or at any rate they had been interned or sentenced by court martial after the Rising was suppressed. It was an opinion often expressed at the time that the convict jails of England were the universities of revolution; not only did Irishmen meet in them who might not otherwise have met, but there were other prisoners of conscience!

Apart from being so much in prison, and therefore the objects for sympathy and admiration, the members of Dáil Éireann had not had a great deal to do with events in Ireland since the Rising. A ground swell of feeling in the country carried the survivors of the Volunteers who fought

11.

in 1916 to the election victory of 1918—but only 30[1] of them to the Mansion House on January 21st, 1919.

Nobody survived the 1916 Rising to take part in Dáil Éireann who had had any important part in creating the literature of the insurrection, or who understood its motives in depth. The men and the parliament which are the subject of this study were filling a gap. They can hardly be said to have had any more previous commitment to revolution, or training for it than any one could have had from the mosquito press, and the pamphlets of the time. Countess Markievicz was the exception.

Larry Ginnell and James O'Mara were the only members of Dáil Éireann who had ever sat in a parliament before. Hardly any of them had been present at constituency conventions either to seek or decline nomination. Likewise few of the constituents who voted for the Republican candidates —'Put him in to get him out'—had had any opportunity to judge the suitability of their men for national politics. Ireland picked her representatives for the first Dáil, and voted for them because they had shown courage and qualities of leadership. For instance, take the case of Eamon de Valera, senior surviving commandant of the Rising. He broke the dread gloom and iron discipline of Dartmoor on the day when he stepped out from a file of Irish prisoners, called the men to attention, and ordered them to salute MacNeill, who was being brought into the wing. The act of a split second had a far reaching effect on de Valera's career and on history. The story went from mouth to mouth everywhere. People were looking for one hero bigger than all the others. From then for a long time they had him.

In the election campaign the Republicans had told the Irish people that its real power was at home in Ireland.

---

1. Concerning the attendance of Michael Collins and Harry Boland at the first meeting there is a conflict between the official report issued by order of the Dáil at the time, and the report which is at present in print. I am supported by Mrs. Geraldine Dillon, and Dr. Eileen McCarville who were present and saw Michael Collins in attendance—or leaving early. The official report, printed by the Liberty Press, gives them both i lathair.

A pamphlet[2] quoted John Dillon in the House of Commons 3rd December, 1917, "Our position in the House is made futile. We are never listened to"; and Mr. Devlin, next day "I do not often come to this House because I do not believe it is worth coming to", and Michael Davitt in 1899 "I have for four years tried to appeal to the sense of justice in this House of Commons on behalf of Ireland. I leave convinced that no just cause, no cause of right, will ever find support from this House of Commons unless it is backed up by force".

The language of the "No Rent Manifesto" of the Land League suited the new situation in its broader appeal; and it served again; against John Dillon, who so many years before had been a signatory of the original document: —

"Against the passive resistance of an entire population, military power has no weapons . . . No power on earth except faint-heartedness on your own part, can defeat you . . . The world is watching to see whether all your splendid hopes and noble courage will crumble away at the first threat of a cowardly tyranny . . . Stand together in the face of the brutal and cowardly enemies of your race . . . Stand passively, firmly, fearlessly, while the armies of England engage in their hopeless struggle against a spirit which their weapons cannot touch . . . The Government will learn how powerless is armed force against the will of a united, determined, and self-reliant nation."

2. The pamphlet quoted is "The Issue". The case for Sinn Fein, by Lector. (New Ireland Pamphlets No. 3). As passed by censor. New Ireland Publishing Co. Ltd., 13 Fleet St., Dublin, 1918.
This firm appears to have developed into "The Liberty Press and Wood Printing Works" which did much of the official printing for the First Dáil Éireann—and may even have belonged to the Dáil, or the I.R.B.
Printers did not continue to be able to put their names on their publications—a fact which adds to the interest of this one.
Information from the late Mr. Paddy S. O Flannagain, former manager and managing director, Liberty Press and Wood Printing Works, and before that editor of "The General Advertiser" and "Irish Opinion". Afterwards editor of "The Plain People"—suppressed by the Free State—and finally editor of "The Derry Journal" from which he retired in 1957.

Reliance on the moral solidarity and economic power of a nation, that was the Sinn Fein appeal. The pamphlet goes on: —

> "Even a small determined minority, if prepared to suffer, can effect enormous reforms. The English Suffragettes have won the franchise for women ... A handful of determined women made government extremely difficult and thus they won the vote in spite of Parliament ... How irresistible would be an entire nation?"

A small minority representation on the Employers' Federation would not serve the workers any more than a minority in the House of Commons can serve Ireland: —

> "The modern Labour movement is based on self-reliance, on the power and cohesion of large numbers, on the slowly built up economic strength of great unions. Sinn Fein is merely the transfer of this faith from Labour to Nationality. That is what we are aiming at in Ireland: the formation of One Big Union ... We must put ourselves in the position of taking over the existing organisations—the parliamentary constituencies, the county and district and municipal councils ... every single body that has a share in directing the national life ...
>
> "Attendance at Westminster is immoral and dishonest ... The members of the Irish Party when seeking election have always indulged in an orgy of sedition ... They tell us the English Government is to be resisted and fought by every means ... Yet how do they take their seats in Westminster and each draw £400 a year? By taking the following oath: —
>
> > "I, John Redmond, do swear that I will be faithful and bear true allegiance to his Majesty, King George V, his heirs and successors, according to law, so help me God".

It had been the aim of Sinn Fein to contest every seat in the whole of Ireland, and to raise again the issue of the United Irishmen, calling on Catholic, Protestant and Dissenter to ratify the independence proclaimed in 1916 in the common name of Irishmen. This was accomplished in part only; it was thwarted, with lasting and fatal effect, in South Armagh, East and South Down, Tyrone N.E., Tyrone S., Monaghan N., Derry S., constituencies where the appearance of a Nationalist candidate maintained a religious confrontation against the Orangemen which Sinn Fein hd hoped to eliminate by previous agreement among all sections which purported to stand already for the freedom of Ireland.[3]

The Nationalists would have had to be bigger men than they were to surrender anything they felt able to fight after reading the Manifesto of Sinn Fein.

The censor deleted large sections of this forcible publication, particularly those in which the Nationalist Party was attacked for their recruiting activities in the war.

"The policy of our opponents stands condemned on any test, whether of principle or expediency. *The right of a nation to sovereign independence rests upon immutable natural law and cannot be made the subject of a compromise.* Any attempt to barter away the sacred and inviolate rights of a nationhood begins in dishonour and is bound to end in disaster. The enforced exodus of millions of our people, the decay of our industrial life, the ever increasing financial plunder of our country, the whittling down of the demands for the 'Repeal of the Union' . . . to Home Rule on the Statute Book, and finally the contemplated mutilation of our country, are some of the ghastly results of a policy that leads to national ruin.

"Those who have endeavoured to harness the people of Ireland to England's war chariot, ignoring the fact that only a freely elected Government in a free Ireland has

3. That this was a reasonable hope was demonstrated in the Nationalists' failure to stand at all in 36 constituencies, involving an almost total collapse in Munster—Cork, Kerry and Clare going whole to Sinn Fein, along with Limerick City and Limerick W. and two Tipperary seats. Outside these Sinn Fein was unopposed in Carlow, Cavan E. and Cavan W., Galway E., Galway S., Kilkenny N., Laoighis, Mayo S., Roscommon N.

See Appendix, Sean T. O'Kelly and Sir James McMahon.

*power to decide for Ireland questions of peace and war,
have forfeited the right to speak for the Irish people.
The Green Flag turned red in the hands of the Leaders.
Ireland must repudiate the men who, in a supreme
crisis for the nation, attempted to sell her birthright for
the vague promises of English ministers, and who showed
their incompetence by failing to have even those
promises fulfilled.*
*"The present Irish members of the English Parliament
constitute an obstacle to be removed from the path that
leads to the Peace Conference . . ."* (suppressed bits in
italics).

It would be a mistake to think that the new men were all
very simple, straightforward idealists. That they were such
was the impression of their followers among the general
public at the time. To anyone reading the manifesto the
opposite thought that divisive politics were any part of
their motive would have been too monstrous to contem-
plate in a country which was still enthralled by the glory,
and the example of 1916. (See note in appendix.)

The approaching decline of the British Empire was a
delightful, bracing, galloping rumour of great value to the
Irish Republic in the days of the first Dáil. It encouraged
old men to persevere in life on earth another year or so,
in the hope that they would live long enough 'to see the
day'; for youth it made the war they were fighting appear
to be a thing which might end in triumph, instead of going
on and on, if necessary for ever and ever, generation after
generation. The time came during the lifetime of the first
Dáil when we seemed to be holding all the cards and
England nothing except the power to go on killing:

"England is beaten, shout we triumphant,
England is beaten; Ireland is free."

No movement which ever arose in Ireland was more
splendidly served by those who adopted its ideals. Patrick
Pearse's appeal for recruits was as relevant in 1919 as it
had been in 1915; but in the later period it was answered
by civilians as well as soldiers, irrespective of age; in fact
by all the types of people who are capable of great and

steadfast courage in national emergency. Every country produces them.

"We want recruits because we have undertaken a service which we believe to be of vital importance to our country, and because that service needs whatever there is of manly stuff in Ireland in order to its effective rendering.

"We want recruits because we have a standard to rally them to . . . There is no other standard in the world so august as the standard we bear; and it is the only standard which the men of Ireland may bear without abandoning their ancient allegiance . . . Ireland as a whole has never fought under any other.

"We want recruits because we have a faith to give them and a hope with which to inspire them . . . The faith is that Ireland is one, that Ireland is inviolate, that Ireland is worthy of all love and all homage and all service that may lawfully be paid to any earthly thing; and the hope is that Ireland may be free. In a human sense, we have no desire, no ambition but the integrity, the honour, and the freedom of our native land . . . We have the strength and the peace of mind of those who never compromise.

"We want recruits because events are about to place the destinies of Ireland in our hands, and because we want as much help as possible to enable us to bear the burden.

"We would band together all men capable of working for Ireland and give them men's work.

"We want recruits because we are absolutely determined to take action the moment action becomes a duty. If a moment comes . . . when the Irish Volunteers will be justified to their consciences in taking definite military action, such action will be taken".

1	**DE MARKIEVICZ.** (Constance De Markievicz, of 143 Leinster Road, Rathmines, Co. Dublin, Married Woman.)	✕
2	**FIELD.** (William Field, of Howth View, Blackrock, Co. Dublin, Gentleman.)	
3	**KELLY.** (James J. Kelly, of 35 Upper Camden Street, Dublin, Tobacco Expert, Alderman, J.P,)	

Countess Markievicz was the first woman to be elected to Parliament in Ireland or England. Dublin gave her a tremendous welcome home from prison. This letter and ballot paper were waiting for her on her release in 1919. "Jan. 1st, 1919. 273192. 51st Labour Company 2 Platoon B.E.F. France. To Mme. Constance de Markievicz. Dear Madam—I wish to draw your attention to the fact that I only received your ballot paper Dec. 31st, too late to vote. I will be very pleased if you will let the public know how the soldiers' vote has been lost. Yours sincerely. Pte. L. Hudson."

RETROSPECT

CHAPTER 2

THE Irish Nation could, and should have established its own Parliament 43 years earlier, in 1876, the time the ballot box was introduced. But the Fenians had shot their bolt, and the prisons were full, and the public mind had turned to London politics. Home Rule was then not long invented. It was unfortunate that Parnell knew no Irish history. His sister, Anna, who did, bridged the years for us in an account which she wrote afterwards: —

"Home Rule was, of course, merely the offering of a compromise by the weaker party to the stronger . . . the principal argument for the change was that it would benefit Ireland; but nobody stated any reason why England would wish to benefit Ireland . . ."

"In Ireland the most important objection advanced against Home Rule was that a scheme which contemplated any connection with England whatever was in itself mischievous . . . Thirty three years of Home Rule propaganda have resulted in a voluntary and deliberate surrender all along the line, to the whole of England's chains and pretensions regarding Ireland, and in a virtual repudiation of Ireland's claim as a right.

"The election of 1876 was the first general election under the Ballot Act. This Act did not diminish bribery in England, but if anything tended to increase it. Its effect in Ireland was very different. The candidate of the two English parties, backed by their hundreds of thousands in ready money, saw themselves ignored and rejected wholesale for the sake of almost penniless men who had nothing except a bare profession of nationalism to offer. How much sacrifice on the part of Irish electors this first Home Rule Party must have involved only those who know the poverty of the Irish people can realise.

"It is a pity not to be able to say that these sacrifices were justified by the Party itself. Unhappily there could not be a greater contrast between the energy of the electors and the apathy of the elected . . ."

The land war, in its various forms, was a much older thing in Irish history than the Republican revolutionary tradition. At all times the dauntless fighting heroes of the Nation have had to be fed by ordinary people—otherwise none of them could have lasted a week after they spent the last of their personal means: heroes perish and in due course are succeeded by younger idealists. But through the greater part of our near 800 years since the invasion, the ordinary man lived off the ground and his need for a place of his own, and security in possession of it, is older than revolution; it is as old as civilisation and nearly as necessary to his neighbours as to himself.

Anna Parnell was the leader of the Ladies Land League. She wrote an account of this period which has never been published. In this extract she shows how things might have developed in 1879 if Mr. Gladstone's government had not arrested some of the Land League leaders and made it impossible for the organisation to function, except through "The Ladies".

It explains perhaps better than has been done elsewhere, why the British arrested Parnell.

Anna Parnell on the duties of government and on virtual assumption of government functions by the Land League:

"In old times the duty of a ruler to protect his subjects from extermination by famine was taken for granted. When Joseph had interpreted Pharoah's dream to him, Pharoah did not talk about political economy, or distributing the balance of economic conditions, or of the laws of supply and demand, but pressed at once to meet the evils foreshadowed by Joseph. That it was only the business of a Pharoah he had no doubt. It is rather interesting to compare the ideas of that old Pharoah with those of Queen Victoria regarding the obligations of sovereigns.

"When O'Connell saw a famine approaching he ran to the English government, like a sheep appealing to a wolf . . . The Young Irelanders wrote poetry.

"The Land League went neither to the English Government nor to the Muses, but set about trying to stop the famines themselves. As rulers are those who rule they become from that moment a government de facto. Had they only continued as they began there might now be only one government in Ireland, and that not English. "In 1847 the tenants sold all they had to pay the landlords and then lay down to die . . .

"When the Famine of 1879-80 became a certainty there seemed to be no lack of energy and decision among the Irish in choosing their part . . . The founding of the Land League in 1879 . . . marked a novel episode in Irish history.

"From that time until the present day there have always been two governments in Ireland, one English, the other Irish, in some sense a Home Rule government.

"The Home Rule League never attempted any of the functions of a government, but the Land League took on a good many of them at once, and all the Nationalist societies which have followed . . . have taken up the same position, more or less.

"In the last 26 years this small, wretched country, so absolutely in the power of her bigger neighbour, has kept up an independent government on voluntary revenues, receiving tribute from its empire beyond the seas, on which the sun never sets.

"The first principle of the Land League was that the cultivator was entitled to the first fruits of his labours, while the landlord was entitled to nothing until the farmers' wants were satisfied. Its ultimate aim was the conversion of the tenants into owners of their holdings . . .

The advice was given to monster gatherings . . . to give no more than they could spare to the landlords after paying their other debts and providing for themselves and their families. The tenants of each estate were told to agree with one another as to what they could offer the landlord and if he refused to accept it as payment in full, to tell him he would get nothing. They were also told that no tenant should make a separate settlement for himself . . . unless all the others were included, even those who might have nothing to offer, the richer tenants thus protecting the poorer. Lastly they were told to discourage 'land grabbing' (taking a farm from which another had been evicted) with all their power.

"This clause was the most important of all because it was clear that a famine could not be caused by high rents unless other tenants could be found to take the evicted farms and pay rents for them.

"To recommend withholding rents and forming combinations between all classes of tenants to stand by each other only for a famine year would only have meant postponing the famine to some other year. The programme of a permanent resistance until the aim of the League should be attained was the only logical one.

"The step the Irish leaders took at this time was the only one open to them, if they intended to effect any reform, but it was a very serious one. It amounted to a defiance of English power. Short of actual war it was the most difficult enterprise possible . . .

"Mr. Gladstone had worked himself into a pathetic and public state of grief and indignation over the sorrows of political prisoners in Italy, but he had yielded to no one in savage treatment of Fenian prisoners when he was in power".

Anna Parnell knew all the complexities and the vast difficulties which had been raised by the Land War, and that the final achievement was much less than the first aims. She in her time was as distressed by the failure of the Home Rule movement as many in our time are because the Proclamation of 1916 has not been implemented.

She was burning with indignation at the methods used against it by the English Government, and the appalling defects in courage and leadership of the parliamentary representatives in the Home Rule Party. If the people had really wanted freedom they might have won it then, she thought. But the evicted did not get the support that was necessary. Land grabbers often got the farms from which public opinion and boycotting should have driven them. Weakness of character, she concluded, had defeated national progress; the landlords had ended with more material wealth than they at first possessed.

She wrote—about 1906—with just indignation and in possession of first hand knowledge.

"Preparations for the future ought to be made. The questions of the early twentieth century promise to be very different for Ireland than those of the 19th. The real opportunity for accomplishing the freedom of Ireland seems to be close at hand, just when her people seem to have put it beyond their power to take advantage of it . . .

"It was customary for public speakers to talk as if the Irish people were perpetually panting to make war on England, and could only be refrained therefrom by the prudence of their leaders . . .

"This kind of talk has now given away to doctrines of the most opposite nature, the popular press seeming nervously anxious to keep the faintest hint that fighting ever had anything to do with a country obtaining independence, from its columns. This change is not a bad sign. The Irish . . . in my recollection, have never done anything when they talked about doing it. Whatever they have done has always been without talk beforehand . . .

"Yet in spite of poor prospects armed rebellion seems to be the next thing either tried, or played at here. The ridicule thrown on rebellion by the Fenian example was enough to put the subject out of court for a long time; but now both Parliamentary proceedings, and such forms of resistance as the Land League proposed have been made equally ridiculous by the way they have been managed, and the Fenian example is furthest away in point of time . . .

"There is another cause that is likely to operate in the same direction. It is the nearness of England's fall. The majority of those now alive will see it . . .

"It is only possible to make small preparations at present. The very first thing that strikes me is to abandon the 'demand' for Home Rule. Continuing to offer a compromise for England's acceptance, after it has been refused for thirty years, is highly undignified on our part. The next offer of compromise ought to come from England.

"To inform her that her government is intolerable, and that Ireland is a separate country by the act of nature, and therefore cannot be well governed except by herself, ought to be quite enough.

"The method of raising Ireland by increasing her wealth through Irish manufacturers, etc., is often spoken of but cannot be counted on unless some one can discover a way for preventing England from taking the profits. All such schemes could only produce results slowly. A sudden rise in wealth, such as the success of the Land League could have brought about, would be the only kind that might enable people to keep and add to the profit they had gained".

Ann Parnell inherited the best Irish Protestant tradition on her father's side, and the brave instinct of republican revolt through her mother, the friend of Fenians, and the daughter of Admiral Stewart of the U.S. Navy, who had helped to establish the freedom of the seas in contest with the British. It is interesting to note the high degree to which she was attuned—perhaps knowingly, perhaps unknowingly—to the religious ideals contained in the Natural Law—but so jealously hidden away from common knowledge. How interesting to note her conception that the struggle of the Land League, in its first stages, was to assert the natural right of human beings not to be deprived of the means of living in peace and dignity following on the unjust distribution of property under English law.

When the time comes that people take as much account of their idealists through history as they do of the opportunist leaders who made the headlines, people like Anna Parnell will be vindicated. The men leaders of the Land League had foreseen that they would be jailed. They created "The Ladies Land League" to take over the Land League offices in their absence. The conflict between idealist and opportunist developed when Parnell compromised with Gladstone's government, and emerged from prison with a new programme.

I have quoted enough of Anna's manuscript to show that she was in front of the elected representatives at that time in her understanding that resistance to oppression could only be worthy and effective when based on the idea of a functioning home government, no matter how hard pressed, or embryonic. Her correct conclusion was that the Home Rule campaigns, when persisted in to the point of national humiliation, amounted to no more than a public demonstration of the slave spirit, which had grown up under the conquest and, as she saw things, would not easily be overcome.

In many ways history was to repeat itself in the following periods.

The Home Rule movement was the worst thing that could have happened after the election of 1876 because enormous changes, which would affect the whole of humanity were taking place and only a home government could have protected the interests of Ireland and her people.

The G.P.O. and Nelson Pillar were both new in 1818 and Irish agriculture—such as it was under the Landlord System —was supplying all the needs of home transport.

The invention of steam power meant that, sooner or later, horse transport would be beaten from the roads, and that coal from England would replace oats and hay. Similarly the cultivation of large tracts of wheat land in North America, and the invention of the roller mill in Austria, resulted in the introduction of white flour and increased imports of foreign wheat. These two events brought agriculture in Ireland to the end of an era, and made it necessary for the British Government to come to the aid of the Irish landlords, who were one arm of its Irish garrison. If one can believe the historians, and also, on a point like this, the Earl of Midleton, leader of "The Southern Unionists", landlord farming had been materialistic. People were a crop to be cultivated or evicted according to the balance of profit between beef and rents.

It was in the people's interest to be a paying crop and, as millions—varying in number from eight to four according as it was fixed by market fluctuations—had no other way to live they were forced to throw in every material thing they had in order to buy that year's permission to work a plot or a farm. This is the reason why so many had only potatoes for their own food and why the change in the transport system mattered so much to so many.[1]

Mr. Gladstone was a very crafty gentleman, and when he introduced the Land Acts he aimed at important objectives which were attained by the British in course of time:

He secured the permanent future of the resident British garrison by giving the Landlords money instead of land; when this money was invested it became, with the men who owned it, part of the continuing 'British interest'.

Classes of farmers and landless men emerged. As the land was parcelled out the Irish were divided into 'haves' and 'have nots'. (The latter included generous and faithful people who had suffered eviction, or come under the notice

---

1. Grain storage barns which still survive are sometimes called 'bottle towers'. It is forgotten that each of these was once the centre of a community which tilled the soil painfully and paid its rents in grain. The barn enabled the landlord to hold the oats or wheat for a rise in price.

of the police for political reasons. It included, too, the young and the old and those who were not judged to be 'credit worthy' claimants for land—many men who were mature in 1912-1922.)

Home Rule, if carried, would, from the British view, transfer vast problems arising with the new industrial age.

The government was not prepared to save its own proletariat from dreadful sufferings—still less did they want to be encumbered with the Irish poor.

Gladstone and Lloyd George in his turn afterwards, persuaded even the Irish of the benevolent intentions and motives of the British government. (Repeated Irish famines and the excesses of government agents in repressing the people, had injured the British image abroad. Their treatment of Ireland was compared with the worst chapters in all history.[2]

None of these achievements availed to obscure the vision and the observations of writers like Henry George or Karl Marx. The example of Ireland under British capitalist rule became an integral part of the literature of world socialism.

The Land War is represented now as having ended in victory for the tenants—as it did for thousands of individuals. In the chorus of approval and newspaper propaganda no voice could compete if it was raised to point out that the Land Commission had been created the Usurper of Divine Powers. The Commissioners scrutinising and deciding on claims for land had no mandate to reinstate the Irish nation or to satisfy justice. So human rights to property which had been good in the tradition of the people since the Plantations were set aside. Solomon could not have wedded justice to the conception of economic holdings for credit worthy wen: many who had borne the heat of the battle, suffered eviction, or otherwise got themselves black listed, failed to be reinstated.

2. The atrocities committed by the British government brought one splendid aspect of British political life: the individual Englishman who stood for justice, even against their own government.

It is impossible to explain the long fight of the Irish for repossession of their country unless we accept that everybody who carried the burden, and was still alive after fighting, would share the victory. That the loss of the Irish land was a collective loss shows up over and over again in Irish and Anglo-Irish poetry : —

"One single foot of land there is not left to us, even as alms from the State; no, not what one may make his bed upon, but the State will accord us the grace—strange! of letting us go safe to Spain to seek adventures!

"They (the English) will be in our places, thick hipped, mocking, after beating us from the flower of our towns. . "These are the people—though it is painful to relate it—

who are living in our white moats . . ."
translation by Douglas Hyde of poem by David O Bruadar.

Even Charles Lever, in a later time and for a different class : —

"Oh, once we were an elegant people
Though now we live in cabins of mud;
The land which you see from the steeple
Belonged to us all from the flood".

And who can better illustrate the nature of the call that went out from the Land League than Fanny Parnell : —

HOLD THE HARVEST

"Now are you men, or are you kine, yet tillers of the soil?
Would you be free, or ever more the rich man's cattle toil?
The shadow on the dial hangs, that points the fatal hour
Now hold your own! or branded slaves, for ever cringe and cower.
The serpent's curse upon you lies—ye writhe within the dust,
Ye fill your mouths with beggars' swill, ye grovel for a crust;

Your lords have set their blood-stained heels upon your
    shameful heads,
Yet, they are kind—they leave you still the ditches for
    your beds.
Oh, by the God who made us all—the seignior and the
    serf—
Rise up! and swear this day to hold your own green
    Irish turf!
Rise up and plant your feet as men where now you crawl
    as slaves,
And make your harvest fields your camps, or make of
    them your graves.
The birds of prey are hovering round, the vultures wheel
    and swoop—
They come, the coronetted ghouls! with drum-beat and
    with troop-
They come, to fatten on your flesh, your children's and
    your wives',
Ye die but once—hold fast your lands, and, if ye can,
    your lives.
Let go the trembling emigrant—not such as he ye need;
Let go the lucre-loving wretch that flies his land for
    greed;
Let not one coward stay to clog your manhood's waking
    power;
Let not one sordid churl pollute the nation's natal hour.
Three hundred years your crops have sprung, by
    murdered corpses fed—
Your butchered sires, your famished sires, for ghastly
    compost spread:
Their bones have fertilised your fields, their blood has
    fallen like rain;
They died that you might eat and live—God! have they
    died in vain?

There was no man or movement to lead the casualties of
the Land War to further effort—after they had failed to
become owners of private property in land. For them it

was the end of hopes which had sustained the whole people since the Flight of the Earls. For the farmers it brought the chance to exist by their own efforts—but in a world which was changing. It brought presently the beginning of organised materialism on the land. A new regiment of 'men of no property' became 'farmers' boys', or turned to the City, or emigrated. This was a hidden tragedy while the fall of Parnell and its consequences were making the news-paper headlines.[3]

3. This in turn created a vast problem which Dáil Éireann was called upon to solve, while at the same time fighting the English.

DUBLIN, CENTRE OF REVOLUTION

CHAPTER 3

SO after being the foreign bridgehead for the control of Ireland for a thousand years from the time of the Norsemen, Dublin emerged as the spiritual capital of Ireland challenging London in the early twentieth century. The stratified society in power, descending in strictly defined precedence from the English Viceroy through Dublin Castle, through lords, gentry and ecclesiastics, through Lieutenants and Custodes Rotulorum of counties, County Court Judges, and chairmen of quarter sessions, clerks of the Crown, and clerks of the Peace, and police and magistrates, were not, for the most part, equipped to read or understand the signs. These people were no mixers. The new spirit of Ireland, sparked variously in Belfast, in Tipperary, in Roscommon, in the Gaeltacht, in Workmen's Clubs, or St. Enda's, or Plunkett House, arose in a society which at least in leisure moments was classless, and this protected it from the class conscious establishments. The suggestion to them that any kind of study was desirable—for adults—was as unwelcome then as it would be to many now. One can therefore understand that the writers, poets, dramatists and revolutionaries who made Dublin the spiritual capital, were for a while at least, protected from any corrupting patronage from Castle or Vice Regal Lodge. Because the study of the language and history of Ireland were abhorrent to the 'ruling class' and their imitators, this made it all the more stimulating and delightful to many others.

When, after the Rising, the British Government instituted an inquest on its own regime in Ireland leading up to that 'disastrous event', Viscount Midleton, an Englishman and absentee Irish landlord, who had been Secretary for War in the Cabinet of Lord Salisbury (1900), was very prominent at this enquiry, after which he was rewarded with an Earldom.[1]

Out of many descriptions of Dublin I select Midleton's, because it is his and serves my purpose: —

'Dublin was left untouched. There at the centre was permanent unemployment, hopeless poverty and housing as bad as any in Europe. Twenty thousand families were living in single rooms. They were ripe for trouble . . . A Lord Lieutenant and Chief Secretary who lived in Dublin had left it untouched . . . It is not too much to say that the state of the Capital made the insurrection of 1916 possible. "The faulty conditions of employment gave scope for the opening steps of anarchy. The attempt by James Larkin to secure better terms for workers, in 1911 . . . brought on a desperate struggle between employers and employed. The sore soon spread".

Every other Irish rising since Hugh O'Neill was quickly suppressed. What had happened after all the years to make the 1916 Rising irrepressible at a time when the national spirit had appeared to be nearer than ever before to total degradation? There were, of course, surface events like the Carson campaign and the delay in implementing Home Rule, and the conscription threat, and the stop of emigration during the war.

The deeper reason was perhaps that a vessel had been filling which over-flowed at the very moment in time when a great generation of men, Clarke, Pearse, Connolly, Ceannt, Plunkett, McDonagh, and MacDiarmuid reached maturity and came together.

The influx of people driven to the city out of the country-side by a variety of causes all evil, had been continuous since the breakdown of the Pale—200 years or more. Many of these were drawn off by emigration, or into the British Army.[2]

1. "Ireland Dupe or Heroine".

2. But even Catholics could make money in limited fields in the city—in the drink trade, or the wool trade, for instance—and some of these turned into rich men without leaving Dublin.

Another category were rebels against authority, and the descendants of rebels, living on, or a little over, the poverty line, whose family experience was retained vividly in mind as far back as the Fenians, the Land League or the Invincibles. Dubliners, the subjects of Midleton's description. The same kind of people, living sometimes in the same streets of old Dublin, had known Dean Swift, and held him for Ireland.[3]

In the days of horse-drawn transport and when all the industries were man-powered and susceptible to the talent of exceptional men of any class, it had been possible to be self-employed in or near the city—and happy enough without being rich. One could live without having by force of circumstances, to be subservient, as country tenants had to be, before the landlord, his agents and his friends and relations. Skin the Goat, although a man of uncommon courage in his own right, belonged to a very large section of the Dublin population who were very risky subjects when industrialisation changed the old way of living and forced them under the discipline of the new factory, railway and tramway managements, where labour was hard, hours interminable, and income pegged. It was a new experience for many who had been born in a precarious semi-freedom enabling them to live on their own wits and skills, to have the profit motive cornered by others.

The new doom which fell on life in the city put no floor under squalor but it put a limit to all the possible rewards which, for so many, had hitherto made effort worth while. During all this long later period of the English trouble leading up to 1916—in the midst of which the Nationalist M.P.s were like men in a quicksand, and William O'Brien gathered strength which might soon have led to him challenging John Redmond—the Gaelic Revival was flowing strongly and, as they said, 'non-politically' at home. It ignored the contemporary controversy, and also the large

3. But the Dublin death rate, and general wastage of people in the despised class was such that it was commonly said, in the early twenties of the century that there was hardly such a person to be found as a Dubliner who could trace his ancestors in the City for three generations, let alone back to the time of the Great Dean.

class of people who preferred, as some do still, to find no good of any kind in Ireland. In a very gentle, civilised way it was a unifying movement.

A common interest in the Irish language brought scholars and peasants and wage slaves into communication with one another, and the traditions which had been handed down from mouth to mouth through the centuries, were sought out. This was done for the purposes of Celtic learning— in which foreigners, Swedes, Germans, French, were also interested, in the persons of eminent professors exploring the Gaeltacht. What was politically important in this development came about when the ancient learning was simplified in the early textbooks of the Gaelic League, and a new interest in their own country was brought to city and country. The Gaelic Athletic Association marched hand in hand; between them the assimilation of Ireland by England was averted.

From the beginning of his political career as socialist organiser in Ireland James Connolly understood the limits of world revolutionary thought as applicable to Ireland. He came here by invitation in 1895, and the next year:— "The Irish Socialist Republican Party was founded by a few workingmen whom the writer had succeeded in interesting in his proposition that the two currents of revolutionary thought in Ireland, the socialist and the national, were not antagonistic but complementary." In both these contexts of revolution Ireland was a mother country.

"The struggle for Irish freedom has two aspects: it is national and it is social. The national ideal can never be realised until Ireland stands forth before the world as a nation, free and independent. It is social and economic because no matter what the form of government may be, as long as one class owns as private property the land and instruments of labour from which mankind derive their substance, that class will always have it in their power to plunder and enslave the remainder of their fellow creatures".

Searching out the labour argument, backwards through Irish history—a formidable task at that stage of Irish scholarship—Connolly found the Brehon Law and the tradition of native culture going back a thousand years before the conquest. He followed the breaking of the Irish system, by methods more subtle and more fatal than arms, in their lasting effect. He drank in the story of ribbonmen and raparee and Ralahine until he was, intellectually, as firmly based on Irish soil as any of his contemporaries who were born and bred here. In his foreword to "Labour in Irish History": —

> "This book, attempting to depict the attitude of the dispossessed masses of the Irish people in the great crisis of modern Irish history, may justly be looked upon as part of the literature of the Gaelic Revival. As the Gaelic language, scorned by the possessing classes, found its last fortress in the hearts and homes of the 'lower orders', so in the words of Thomas Francis Meagher, the same 'wretched cabins have been the holy shrines in which the traditions and hopes of Ireland have been treasured and transmitted'."

Connolly and his family were driven out by hunger in 1903 but it should be remembered that during the first phase of his political activity in Ireland Tom Clarke was still doing his terrible sentence of penal servitude, and Patrick Pearse had not yet started his school.

The Gaels were now drawn from all Ireland and the Protestants among them constituted a new generation of men and women of alien ancestry, in some cases, but patriot strain. Some, like W. B. Yeats, started revolution but did not see it through. The actresses who reached distinction in the early history of the Abbey Theatre were drawn from Inghinidhe na hEireann, the revolutionary woman's organisation founded by Maud Gonne; some of them were prominently associated with the terrible struggle for human rights which had its centre a few blocks away in Liberty Hall, under James Larkin and James Connolly. The Abbey Company which brought "Kathleen ni Houlihan" abroad to London put their own revolutionary spirit into the parts they acted, and the cause of "the Four Green Fields" of Ireland turned boys and girls—exiled Irish— into the service of their own country.

This was all too wide based not to be vulnerable. The first break was chiselled by Irish hands when the political Party, largely owned by the Ancient Order of Hibernians, moved to control the Irish Volunteers, split them, and took a very large proportion of the members.

The fracture which followed went into every section of the Revival and was driven from London. "Your King and Country Need You" was proclaimed from every notice board—outside police barracks, in all railway stations, on every available blank wall—while the British and French Armies retreated from Mons at the outset of the world war, and during its duration, 1914-18.

John Redmond, M.P., leader of the Parliamentary Party, joined the recruiting drive. Redmond exhausted himself in the long effort to keep the British Government to its legal and fully official commitment to Home Rule.

Connolly put a streamer across the front of Liberty Hall. "WE SERVE NEITHER KING NOR KAISER BUT ONLY IRELAND". After the split from the Redmondites there remained no important difference involving national principle between the men who were soon to be comrades in the leadership of the Insurrection. It only remained for the secret revolutionary movement and the open Socialist revolutionary movement to decide how they should work together for the common objective.

It is Ireland's misfortune that the solution did not outlive the men who made it, and implemented it at Easter, 1916. By 1916 many thousands of nationalist Irishmen had been enticed to join the British army in the war against Germany. Home Rule had been passed through all stages, and was on the Statute Book, to be implemented after the war. Some poor men went in the spirit of soldiers of freedom whose own country was now safe. It was "little Belgium" which needed to be rescued from Germany. Green flags appeared. In the composition of these the Harp was surmounted by the Crown, and in the top right hand corner was a Union Jack!

Soon it was made plain that even this was not a true symbol of what was to be expected. England made her first move to implement the partition of Ireland. Carson's Ulster Volunteers were made into a separate Division, an "honour" not accorded to the other, much larger sections of Irish-British soldiers; Edward Carson, after breaking all the laws that suited him in the Orange campaign, became Attorney General for England—soon to be brought into the British War Cabinet.

The certainty grew that Irishmen not willing to volunteer for the English war would soon be forced to go, under conscription. The time during which their lives would be their own was diminishing rapidly. It was plain to every man that his certain fate was to be a soldier. He was bound to ask himself "on which side?"

The structure of British Government in Ireland had not varied from the Land League to the Rising, except that D.O.R.A., the Defence of the Realm Act added such things as the censorship, rationing, restrictions of lighting, and on movement iside and out of the country, etc., from 1914 on. There never had been any constitutional method of asserting the public will, except in the House of Commons where the Irish were outnumbered by more than six to one; now there were additional petty restrictions. It was in this setting the next chapter opened.

Pearse and Connolly, and the men who rose with them, were convinced that a protest in arms was the only possible measure within their power to take, if the complete destruction of the Irish nation was to be averted. The arguments which support their view are in the writings of the men; and the conclusions they drew are expressed in the aims of the Rising, and the guarantees which are in the text of their Proclamation.

The War of Independence which followed was only good and holy to the extent that the cause was unadulterated by selfishness at later stages.

Put the Proclamation beside the ecumenical, and social principles which are studied so keenly to-day, and we who fought for the Irish Republic in good faith can hold our heads high. What Pearse and Connolly proclaimed was consistent with God's Law.

It will be my submission that no such claim can be advanced on behalf of either government operating in Ireland to-day. While something called Freedom was won—on both sides of the Border, the aims and objects of the fight were lost. Materialism took over.

If this were not so human rights would not be flouted in both areas.

The natural right of every adult human being of good will to have the opportunity to make a living, marry, raise children, and have a dignified life, would not be subordinated to lower, materialistic interests. It would have been acknowledged and implemented two or three generations ago. Children would be brought up in an atmosphere of security, with roots in their own country; the earnings of one parent would be enough to provide for a family.

I would not be forced to write that the fight for the rights of the Irish people to ownership of Ireland and their own souls is as good, and holy, and necessary to-day as it was in 1916, or a century ago, in the time of Michael Davitt. The Proclamation, as everyone knows, or should know, was issued on Easter Monday, 1916, "In the name of God and of the dead generations". In the name of Ireland it guaranteed "Religious and civil liberty, equal rights and equal opportunities to all citizens" and declared its "resolve to pursue the happiness and prosperity of the whole nation and all its parts, cherishing all the children of the nation equally, and oblivious of the differences carefully fostered by an alien government, which have divided a minority from the majority in the past".

The Proclamation placed "the cause of the Irish Republic under the protection of the Most High God, whose blessing we invoke upon our arms, and we pray that no one who serves that cause will dishonour it by cowardice, inhumanity, or rapine. In this supreme hour the Irish Nation must, by its valour and discipline and by the readiness of its children to sacrifice themselves for the common good, prove itself worthy of the august destiny to which it is called".

The 1916 leaders justified their first aim, to strike for

freedom, by their intention to secure human rights, when they had attained the power to do so. It is my purpose in other essays, to examine the reasons why the guarantee in the Proclamation was not honoured in the fifty years since then, because a just society was incompatible with the continuing British interest.

Father Martin has suggested that the appeal of Pearse was most powerful in the years subsequent to his death, and that of Connolly grew stronger at a much later time.

This may be true enough in the sense that Pearse was a school master and understood the youthful mind. The six day defence of the Tricolour Flag, planted on the chosen Dublin buildings, the hoof-clatter of the Lancers' loose horses in O'Connell Street, the battle at Ashbourne, above all the defence of Mount Street Bridge by a handful of volunteers against an English battalion, turned a significant number of young people into citizens from the moment they witnessed, or read of these events.

The lesson in their history books that risings only happened long ago, and were now neither possible nor desirable, were contradicted dramatically. The murders in North King Street, and of Francis Sheehy-Skeffington; the executions, particularly those of James Connolly, thought to be wounded to death anyhow, and Willie Pearse—who had no major responsibility for anything that happened—these things brought the older people in and added fuel to the blaze, but did not start it.

The Proclamation raises questions of conscience which touch us at individual level, because no democratic institution of government existed on Easter Monday. The 1916 men depended therefore on their comrades who would survive, and those who would in future embrace their cause, to make the dream come true. The unity of the forces which took part in the Rising was intended to be a permanent comradeship extending from the I.R.B. to the Labourmen of the Citizen Army. It was an act of faith in the inherent nobility of the human soul requiring a continuing capacity for unselfish effort. It nearly came off— the rank and file thought it was effective during the next twenty years (some may think so still). Over the longer period it became evident that men often do the same things for different reasons, that visions fade, and poems and pamphlets go out of print. Hunger and ambition put up formidable arguments.[4]

Colonel Maurice Moore—that good old man—had spent Christmas, 1916, in the West, and afterwards travelled around to make his own survey of the state of the public mind. He was the military leader of the National Volunteers, so he had all the contacts he needed. His letters can be studied in the National Library. In a number of these he described the change which had come over the nation to John Dillon, M.P. His conclusion was that the Irish Parliamentary Party would not survive the next election.

The Ireland described by Moore was unaffected by the personal presence of men who had taken part in the Rising, for the first releases of internees came at Christmas and it was not usual for released prisoners to take the field again before having a short rest in their homes—it happened very frequently that this was the only opportunity an advanced republican might get to meet his family because he would so soon be a candidate for re-arrest.

The election of Count Plunkett in North Roscommon confirmed the Colonel's opinion.

The first Easter Commemoration—and the most stimulating ever to be held—was carried out by the Citizen Army. (According to the late Mr. Bouch's study of the second printing of the Proclamation of Easter Week, the planning was done mainly by a group of women members—led by Helena Molony, Connolly's trusted assistant, who had been released from prison at Christmas.) "Easter was an occasion of fearless demonstration of adherence to the insurgents' memory, and their cause . . . The tide of enthusiasm was rising steadily, a powerful force, as yet unharnessed and uncontrolled", wrote Dorothy Macardle.

4.   The old unity thrilled again when left, right and centre came together to organise resistance to conscription; but, so far as any public manifestations went we know now that it ended with the end of the world war—November 11th, 1918, fifty years ago.

Following on the Roscommon Election, and the Easter Commemoration, and the formation of Liberty Clubs under Count Plunkett's leadership, and the Longford Election—another victory—came the Plunkett Convention. It brought evidence that the republican-socialist partnership of Easter Week was about to be renewed. The Labour movement and the Citizen Army were there and also the most active and most efficient and far reaching organisation of the period. This was the Republican Prisoners' Dependants' Fund, which on April 18th, accounted for £107,069, collected inside the year, and being dispensed all the time in relief.

Griffith, hoping to steal the revolution for his own restricted ideals, and the unreformed Sinn Fein, was short of supporters.

But invitations to the Convention had been sent on an over optimistic scale and reached timid men. The meeting ended in confusion and a joint committee was left to decide upon the next moves.[5]

It could be argued that the British Government moved with unerring instinct to benefit from a temporary confusion and help towards the most conservative possible sequence. They released Eoin MacNeill who had counterordered the Rising, and with him the remaining penal servitude prisoners.

It must have been as clear to the English authorities as it was to observers in Ireland that the national spirit of the men in jail was greatly strengthened in response to every news which reached them of the response of the nation at home to their sacrifice. Every letter erased some of the memory of their humiliation after the surrender under the jeers, in some streets, of watching crowds as they were escorted to the cattle boats for shipment in some cases to undergo life imprisonment.

5. The Convention called by Count Plunkett, T.D., N. Roscommon, met April 19th, 1917, and adjourned to September. The Convention called by Mr. Lloyd George, which was presided over by Sir Horace Plunkett, first met on July 25th, the same year. The final report is dated 5th April, 1918. The penal servitude prisoners were released mid-June, 1917.

Leading personalities of Sinn Fein 1916-'21

Front: *Mrs. Aine Ceannt,* widow of the 1916 leader, Vice-President Cumann na mBan, afterwards secretary of the Children's Committee of the Irish White Cross. *Eamon Duggan, T.D.,* plenipotentiary in London, 1921. *Dr. Kathleen Lynn,* medical officer, Irish Citizen Army, 1916; co-founder of St. Ultan's Baby Hospital; untiring worker to improve the social services under the Dáil. *Arthur Griffith,* Acting President, Irish Republic, in absence of the President. *Eamon de Valera,* President Dáil Éireann, April 1919, President Irish Volunteers, 1917, President National University. *Michael Collins,* Minister of Finance; Head of the I.R.B.; Director of Intelligence; Plenipotentiary, London, 1921. *Harry Boland, T.D.,* Joint hon. secretary, Sinn Fein; prominent in Bond drive in U.S.A.; envoy of the Irish Republic to Washington after return of President de Valera to Ireland, December, 1920. *Mrs. Hanna Sheehy-Skeffington,* widow of Francis Sheehy Skeffington, who was murdered by British army captain Bowen Colthurst, Easter 1916; champion of Woman's Rights, founder member of Irish Women's Franchise League; Sinn Fein Executive; Member Dublin Corporation. She was the only Irish representative who succeeded in interviewing President Wilson. Second row: *Mrs. Jenny Wyse Power,* member of the Ladies Land League with Anna Parnell; Executive of Cumann na mBan; joint hon. treasurer Sinn Fein; member Dublin Corporation; the Proclamation of 1916 is said to have been signed in her house. *Desmond Fitzgerald, T.D.,* Minister for Propaganda. *Darrell Figgis* is the bearded figure; author, journalist, chancer, joint hon. sec. Sinn Fein; secretary to the Dáil Commission on the Industrial Resources of Ireland; a very competent man; for some proofs of his treachery consult the report of the Broadcasting Commission, 1924. *Kevin O'Sheil, B.L.,* judge in the Dáil Courts. *Austin Stack, T.D.,* Minister for Home Affairs; member of de Valera's inner cabinet; G.A.A.; Gaelic League. *Dr. T. Dillon, D.Sc.,* lecturer in Chemistry, U.C.D.; a member of the committee resulting from Count Plunkett's convention (1917); for a time hon. sec. Sinn Fein; afterwards Professor U.C.G. Back row: *Sean Milroy. Ald. Walter Cole,* whose house, 3 Mountjoy Square, was the most usual meeting place of Dáil Éireann after the British occupied the Mansion House with military force. Last on left: *Paudeen O'Keeffe, T.D.,* secretary of Sinn Fein. (Can anyone supply the names of the others?).

Whether planned or unplanned there can be no doubt that the 'unharnessed and uncontrolled" era came to an end when conservatives gained control of the political revolution.

Speaking in the Second Dáil, nearly five years later, Mr. de Valera told how it had been his aim as leader to hold the balance between Griffith and Brugha. In this connection he made no mention of the ideals of the Rising, or the partnership of Pearse and Connolly.

The counter revolution, within the republican movement, began in October, 1917. Sinn Fein reactionaries included Michael Collins—a thing which no-one could have guessed at the time—who with de Valera and Griffith made the Triumvirate of men with limited objectives which cornered the "republican" leadership—and even held it to personal allegiances after they quarrelled in 1921. (See Appendix).

Griffith stepped in behind de Valera when the (new) Sinn Fein Constitution was stretched to provide the escape clause. Padraig Colum, in his biography put it: "in other words, when, as an act of piety, the aspiration of the insurrectionists was formally honoured, the Irish people might vote for something other than a Republic".

The contest for the allegiance of the people went on everywhere. Picture Daithi Ceannt, of Bawnard, Castlelyons, Co. Cork, not long released from prison, in the fair of Fermoy—he told this himself at an Ard Fheis of Sinn Fein. The police were watching him and his friends; and he and his scouts were watching them. Daithi could not "do his business' in the fair because he was followed everywhere by a police spy. But he was not to be defeated so easily as that: he started to follow the District Inspector wherever he went in the fair: stalemate was reached. The Inspector turned on Daithi: "Why do you follow me?" Daithi pointed to the spy: "For the same reason that he follows me. Call him off and I will have my own business to do". So everyone going home from that fair carried a story, and perhaps, if he needed a lesson, had learned one. He might even have had business to do with Daithi, and have done it.

The weakness was there, indeed; but to the inexperienced multitude of the young and eager it was not apparent because the idealistic statement of war aims by President Wilson had been made familiar everywhere in the recruiting propaganda. If even England stood over these principles of behaviour, were Irish Republicans likely to fall behind? The Freedom of Small Nations; the Sanctity of Treaties; the right of all peoples to have the government of their choice: Open Agreements openly arrived at, these were the modern things which must count, and would prevail. It seemed that Wilson had fallen in between Pearse and Connolly. In whatever decisions the future might hold we were certain to have a vote, and it would be for the Republic already proclaimed, and for nothing less!

Authority was given to this conviction when the first Dáil Éireann ratified the Act of the Provisional Government of 1916 and gave us three fundamental documents: —The Declaration of Independence; the Address to the Free Nations of the World, and the Democratic Programme. No significance was attached at the time to the absence of the Triumvirate; Griffith and de Valera were in prison again, and Michael Collins had gone to Lincoln to rescue "Dev".

Writing from prison before polling day to James O'Mara, fourth Director of the Elections (the others having been arrested) de Valera gave this private hint regarding his attitude to abstention: — "Try to get the election issue kept close to the real point. Abstention is only a corollary". (The previous year he had read the Proclamation of Republic from his election platform in Ennis.)

The English attitude to Ireland at the end of the first world war astonished and outraged a great number of men who had served the King in various capacities. It made Irish soldiers returning from Allied service in the battle-fields of Flanders, reach for their guns again and plead for admission to the Irish Volunteers. It destroyed the Parliamentary Party and helped the victory of Sinn Fein. Never before had the wise old men passing on traditional warnings about Saxon guile been guilty of under-statement in their predictions to the degree now experienced.[6]

Asquith, who had been blamed greatly for stopping the executions after 1916, and Edward Carson, who also disliked them, and who had been willing to preserve the unity of Ireland in return for conscription, had long before given place to tougher men at the head of English politics.

No Irishman was in Lloyd George's Coalition which—if you exclude 73 Sinn Feiners who, of course, never went to Westminster—had a majority of 322, over 156 in the House of Commons after the 1918 election; but Carson's "galloper", F. E. Smith, Lord Birkenhead, was now Lord Chancellor of England. He knew as much as any of them wanted to know about Ireland.

The old disputes between English parties over English policies like Home Rule, ended now. The ranks closed in face of the new Irish demand.

It must be admitted that the English feelings, arising from no matter which degree of materialist society, were no more than human; Ireland was a subject on which the public was very badly informed or very careful misinformed!

The English had come through the greatest war the world had ever known, and for the first time in history bombs had fallen on their island, hitherto secure from anything like that. Everywhere families had lost their children, or children their fathers. Women who had never known what it was to have to work had staffed the factories and toiled in the fields. Everyone, almost, had gone short of food; those accustomed to driving had to walk; people who had

---

6. It was generally accepted elsewhere that "the war had changed everything", but that did not happen here, where no British promise was honoured. The determination to hang the Kaiser died; but it became ever clearer that the men "born to rule" us had survived in London and that the experience of the greater war had hardened and made them into a team. Their determination to settle the affairs of Ireland from the House of Commons was inflexible. "No British Government can barter away the allegiance of British subjects. No British Government can barter portions of Empire. No British Government will coerce Ulster". (Chamberlain.)

never rubbed shoulders had had to rub them. Thousands and thousands of people blamed Ireland for their great troubles. She had stabbed the Empire in the back. When King and country needed the Irish they hung back. Everything that England ever did for Ireland was met with ingratitude. They were given Home Rule and they were not satisfied. They wanted a republic now. Was the Pope to be allowed to rule over the loyal men of Ulster? The Irish had delayed the entry of the United States into the war as England's ally; they had almost prevented that decision; what might they not do next time. The Irish were feckless and unreliable and their wretched country was poor—a bog where the rain never stopped from falling. Catholic countries were all ignorant and backward, and this one more than most.

This was talk which could be heard in Dublin and in the mansions of the Anglo-Irish, too. It was Ireland's misfortune that she has always, for centuries past, had to carry a considerable minority of people who believed the rest of us to be a little less than human. These were the 'West British', the 'Castle Catholics', the professional hereditary soldiers, from private to General, retired, or reservists, drawing their permanent incomes from the ancient enemy of the race, whose sworn servants the military men among them were. In view of their history, their wealth and possessions, and the state of education in their time, it was to be expected that these people would be arrogant, and many of them very, very cruel.

In the days and the years of the great rally following the Rising Irish republicans had little notion of the great load of doubters and active enemies they would have to carry inside Ireland.

At headquarters of Empire the average voter was as unlikely as the average share-holder in a prosperous firm, to show curiosity or interest about the management of his handsome estate, or the sources of his comfortable, and secure living. The corrupt and opportunist government of Mr. Lloyd George—which was to make £3 million a man out of the sale of peerages—got a completely free hand to exercise power politics in the foreign affairs of country and Empire.

President Wilson had hoped to give the world a code for civilised diplomacy—"Open Agreements Openly Arrived At"—to put beside the "Code for Civilised War" which already existed in name.

On November 5th, the week before the armistice (November 11th, Poppy Day!) "the Germans were informed that the Allied Governments were willing to make peace on the terms of the Fourteen Points and the principles enunciated in Wilson's subsequent addresses." (A. J. P. Taylor).
But Wilson, who had saved the English and French from defeat by the Germans in 1916, was the first casualty of the peace. No other world statesman was ever so rebuffed by his dependants at a moment when he arrived as guest on their territory.

"The subject of a World League of Nations seemed for a time to appeal right over the heads of the governments to the peoples of the world. Unhappily President Wilson had to deal with governments instead of peoples ... There was not a single government in the Old world willing to waive one iota of its sovereign independence to attain any such end", wrote H.G. Wells.

This British team, which between them possessed craft and overpowering ability, enough to keep England in power politics long after the decline of her physical strength, was the one against which the government of Dáil Éireann would have to sustain Ireland's claim to be a free and independent nation, acknowledging no other rule than that of its own elected government.

The ideologies were utterly at variance and once the Fourteen Points were thrown overboard there remained no common point of agreement from which the natural rights, and just demands of Ireland—or indeed any other small country might be developed.

When Cathal Brugha had been chosen to be Ceann Comhairle at the opening meeting of the Dáil his first words were a reminder that the work they were about to do that day was more pressing than anything which had been done in Ireland from the time when the English came to the country, and the holiest work. We are people who hope in God; people who respect the laws of God, and because of that it is right that we should pray for God's help to enable us to do this work.

GOVERNMENT ESTABLISHED

CHAPTER 4

"LORD FRENCH is to-day the absolute master of Ireland. He alone, always in consultation with his Chief Secretary, will decide upon the type of government the country is to have, and it is he, rather than any member of the House of Commons, who will be the judge of political and industrial reforms ... The programme for administration has been practically settled".

The paper from which I quote this was on sale in the streets as people left after the Dáil meeting. But those who queued up, with official tickets from their T.D.s, to admit them to the Mansion House, and also the crowd outside who could not be accommodated, cared nothing about Lord French, or the King of England, or anybody connected with them. No day that ever dawned in Ireland had been waited for, worked for, suffered for like that January Tuesday.

People waiting asked one another "Did you ever think you and I would live to see this day?"

I was with a Wexford contingent.

Never was the past so near, or the present so brave, or the future so full of hope.

We filed into the Round Room and pressed around till every inch of standing room was full.

I don't believe I even saw the seating arrangements that first day, the crowd was so great.

We did see Cathal Brugha presiding and we repeated the words of the Declaration after him, and felt we had burnt our boats now. There was no going back.

"Aontuighimid an Fháisnéis Neamh-spleadhchuis seo, agus cuirimid Sinn Fein fa gheasaibh ár ndicheall do dhéanamh chun í chur i bhfeidhm ar gach slighe ar ár gcumas."

Cathal said they were met to do the most important work that had been done in Ireland since the foreigners landed. The people of Ireland hoped and trusted in God, and for that reason they would humbly ask God to give them help in the work they had undertaken.

He then asked "the most faithful priest who had ever lived in Ireland", Father Michael O'Flanagan, to ask the blessing of the Holy Spirit on their work.

Then we saw Father Michael's head and shoulders as he came forward, and our prayer went up with his.

The Dáil met at 3.30. It rose at 5.20, the day's work nobly done.

Some 69 press men from home and oversease reported the proceedings.

Outside, Dawson Street was thronged. Volunteers controlled the crowds, but reinforced D.M.P. (Dublin Metropolitan Police) kept the trams moving. Young people were perched at every point of vantage.

Col. Wedgeworth Johnstone, C.B., Chief Commissioner, D.M.P., and Sir Joseph Byrne, Inspector-General of the R.I.C., were in windows overlooking the street. Detectives were also busy.

A secret instruction went out from the Castle:

"Press Censor to all Irish newspapers: —The Press are informed with reference to the Dáil Éireann Assembly, which was held in the Mansion House, Dublin, on January 21, that the following are not for publication:

1. The Democratic Programme.

2. The Declaration of Independence.

3. Speeches of the proposer and seconder of the Declaration of Independence."

Secret printing presses all over the city pounded out the banned literature.

At least one man put his name to the official translations of the forbidden documents. He was Fergus O'Connor.

There was no difficulty in obtaining any document which the Dáil wanted to distribute. The material sold like hot cakes from under the counters everywhere.

The British were able to maintain their press censorship. It lasted until August, 1921.

The Evening Telegraph in a leader on January 22, 1919, said:

> "Ireland has reached a momentous crisis in her history ... It is neither fair to the people nor to their elected representatives that the Republican programme and the methods by which it is sought to carry it out should be concealed from them by the Press Censor".

The Belfast Newsletter—same date:

> "Owing to the censorship restrictions we cannot print the Declaration as its publication is prohibited".

Telegraph—January 22:

> "His Honour County Court Judge Brereton Barry, K.C., sat at Bray to-day. To one of the solicitors he made a request to conduct his case according to the English Law.

> "The laws of England may be revoked by Proclamation in this country, but at least till we get official knowledge of it we shall have to follow them".

The first Dáil had six session in 1919: the first on January 21 and 22 (private). The Second Session was also private, on April 1, 2, 4, 10 and 11.

The note of proceedings on the last day of the session was destroyed owing to enemy action.

Third Session—May 9 (public) attended by delegates from the United States.
Fourth Session: June 17, 18, 19 (all private).
Fifth Session: August 19 and 20 (private).
Sixth Session: October 27 (private)

In 1920: First Session—June 28 (private); Second Session —August 6 (private); Third Session—September 17 (private).

In 1921: First Session, January 21, 25; Second Session, March 11; Third Session, May 10.

Meeting places of Dáil Éireann, even after it was suppressed, were: The Oak Room, Mansion House; Alderman Cole's house, 3 Mountjoy Square.

It was expected from the very first day that the Dáil would be attacked by the British. Precautions were taken so that everybody would not be captured. Dublin Mansion House is a place with many secrets, and it provided escape routes, which had been fully explored; an emergency drill was ready to go into operation by picked men, to get the leaders out if necessary.

From the beginning, the Dáil was jealous of its dignity and responsibilities: obviously the Ceann Comhairle, Cathal Brugha, would have to stand his ground and could then leave unobtrusively. But Count Plunkett and Eoin MacNeill—next day to be made Minister for Foreign Affairs and Finance—were civilians and could give no better service than by completing their work and leaving by the front door.

Even then it was considered that Michael Collins was the first man the British would want to get. He was present He left early; the same applied to Harry Boland. They went to England that night and therefore must have been really absent at the second meeting of the session, next day, in the Oak Room. It was at this meeting that Cathal Brugha announced the names of his four Ministers—the fourth was National Defence—R. Mulcahy.

That Collins became Minister for Home Affairs is perhaps significant. It was typical of him to be a quick and competent starter on any enterprise. His first duty, and the first concern of the Dáil, was to secure the free access of such members as were then in prison. For this there was no absolute necessity to ask permission of His Majesty's Government.

Members of the first Dáil Éireann who attended the April Session.

Eamon de Valera, Count Plunkett, and Arthur Griffith had no sooner been nominated as delegates to the Peace Conference than Collins proceeded on jail breakings.

"Of the three you are aware that two are in Saxon prisons: the English may think badly of them, but that is not the case with the Gael, and it is my opinion that we could not send three more suitable men to the Peace Conference", said Padraig O Maille when he proposed the names immediately following the Declaration of Independence. De Valera, Sean McGarry, Sean Milroy and Robert Barton were rescued before the April session—as well as a considerable number of republicans who were not T.D.s —Joe McGrath escaped January 23rd. In a face-saving operation the British government made a general release of the untried, and Arthur Griffith, Countess Markievicz, W. T. Cosgrave, Dr. Richard Hayes, Dr. Brian Cusack, and Joseph McGuinness immediately swelled the Dáil numbers. Sean Etchingham, released sick from Lincoln, in January, had brought information which helped the escape from that prison. Piaras McCann, T.D., died in prison. It is difficult to trace now who was "in" and who was "out" at any particular date; for instance Piaras Beaslai and J. J. Walsh who escaped over the wall of Mountjoy Jail in March, had been present at the Dail's first meetings. Their brief spell of imprisonment on that occasion did not interrupt their Dáil attendances.

Austin Stack, for whom the Ministry of Home Affairs was held in de Valera's first cabinet, suffered a long and very grim imprisonment in Belfast and other jails until he was rescued in broad daylight from Strangeways Prison, Manchester, in 1920. He took the Oath of Allegiance to the Republic on June 29th in that year.

Te second session opened in high good spirit, with fifty two members present. Those attending for the first time were breathing the air of freedom after long imprisonment. Cathal Brugha's Ministers read their departmental reports and the formal adoption was passed in one motion: Proposed by Arthur Griffith; seconded by Terence MacSwiney.

There was discussion of Standing Orders and Constitution. The Cathal Brugha tendered his resignation and that of his Ministry, which, after a vote of thanks had been proposed by A. Griffith, and seconded by Eamon de Valera, and passed with acclamation, was accepted.

"On the motion of Cathal Brugha, seconded by P. O Maille, Eamon de Valera was declared elected Priomh-Aire".

The second day of the second session brought men into Irish history, some of whom would hold the stage, for good or ill, during many years. Mr. de Valera nominated his Ministry:—

Secretary for Home Affairs—Arthur Griffith
Secretary for Defence—Cathal Brugha
Secretary for Foreign Affairs—Count G. N. Plunkett
Secretary for Labour—Countess Markievicz
Secretary for Industries—Eoin MacNeill
Secretary for Finance—Michael Collins
Secretary for Local Government—Liam Cosgrave.
Heads of Departments:
   Propaganda—L. Ginnell
   Agriculture—R. C. Barton

The Dail discussed the payment of Ministers at the rate of £1,000 a year for the President and not more than £500 for the other Ministers—depending on the amount of time each would be prepared to give to his official work. Cathal Brugha, the proposer "mentioned" that as he himself could not give all his time to his official duties he would accept no stipend, he would suggest that a substitute for him would be paid £300 per annum".

A select committee was appointed to consider this matter:—Cathal Brugha, Joe MacDonagh, M. Staines, J. Dolan, J. MacGuinness, L. de Roiste, Ald. T. Kelly, E. Blythe.

Other Committees were appointed on the motion of the Home Secretary to consider the East Tipperary vacancy—owing to the death in prison of Pierce McCann, and to report on the imprisonment of absent deputies and other

Prisoners of War, and as to children kidnapped by English agents.

A committee was appointed to assist the Minister for Local Government in preparing policy for his department: — Alderman Tom Kelly, Dr. Hayes, Dr. J. Ryan, J. J. Clancy, F. Fahy, A. O'Connor, F. Lawless, J. J. Walsh, J. Dolan, J. MacGuinness.

The first money to be handled on behalf of Dáil Éireann was a loan of £2,000 put up by Miss Anna O'Rahilly, the sister of the O'Rahilly, in January.

In April Michael Collins was given full power to raise a loan and "without further reference to Dáil to receive all moneys which he can obtain from the proceeds of Anti-Conscription refunds, the issue of Republican Bonds, and all other sources for the purposes of Dáil, and to apply those monies to such specific objects as the Ministry (when not reduced below five in number) shall unanimously approve".

The next day's business included replies to questions by Griffith, that the establishment of public arbitration Courts was planned, and that the Director of Agriculture would submit a report about increased tillage to next session. Earnest Blythe was made Director of Trade and Commerce (Later, when Mr. de Valera went to America, Mr. Blythe was given cabinet rank temporarily.)

The Select Committee to consider payment of Ministers recommended £500 for the Prime Minister and £300 each for Ministers. The Dáil divided on an amendment and finally settled to give the P.M. £600 and Ministers up to a maximum of £350.

On the motion of Eoin MacNeill, seconded by A. Mac-Cabe, the Dáil stated its position on Freedom of the Seas:
"We recognise that on the independence of Ireland more than on any other single fact the Freedom of the Seas depends. It will never be with the consent of the Irish Nation that their land, its coasts and harbours, shall be made use of by any Power to dominate the ocean, which should be a free highway for all peoples. We desire that our ports and harbours should be equally accessible to

all external nations, and that the present naval and mercantile monopoly over them exercised by England to our great detriment and the detriment of other nations shall be abolished."

The Question was put and agreed to.

A proposal, by A. MacCabe and Countess Markievicz "That this Assembly pledges itself to a fair and full redistribution of the vacant lands and ranches of Ireland among the uneconomic holders and landless men.[1]
"That no purchase by private individuals of non-residential land in the Congested Districts, or other land essential for carrying out of any such schemes of land settlement as the Dáil may decide upon, which has taken place since Easter Monday, 1916, be sanctioned now or subsequently by the Irish Republican Government. That this resolution be taken as conveying a warning to those who have recently availed themselves of the crisis in national affairs to annex large tracts of land against the will and interests of the people".

After discussion this resolution was withdrawn. A committee was appointed to consider land policy under the Land Department:—P. O Maille, J. J. Clancy, Alasdair MacCabe, L. Ginnell, D. O Buachalla, P. Moloney, S. Etchingham, E. J. Duggan, J. MacGrath, J. A. Burke.[1]

In a second great public meeting in the Round Room, on April 10th, Mr. de Valera made his first important statement as President:—

1. The Land policy of the First Dáil, and the efforts made to implement it, caused the first serious internal problem. A great deal of space in the report of proceedings is taken up with Land and Agriculture; and the final reports were presented after the Truce, of July 11th, 1921—these are in the official report of Second Dáil. A National Land Commission, and the National Land Bank were established, and progress was made with the acquisition and distribution of Land. But the best that could be done was far less than the demand. Some hungry and desperate men rejected all proposals that they should register claims and recognise the authority and good will of the Dáil. There was already turmoil in parts of the West when Austin Stack escaped from jail in August, 1920. This subject needs a great deal more study than I would be competent to undertake.

"Our first duty as the elected government of the Irish People will be to make clear to the world the position in which Ireland now stands.

"There is in Ireland at this moment only one lawful authority, and that authority is the elected Government of the Irish Republic".

He employed the noble words which Cardinal Mercier had used of Belgium under the Germans: —

"The authority of that power is no lawful authority. Therefore in soul and conscience the Irish people owe that authority neither respect, nor attachment, nor obedience . . .

"Our attitude towards the powers that maintain themselves here against the express will of the people shall in a word, be this. We shall conduct ourselves towards them in such a way as will make it clear to the world that we acknowledge no right of theirs . . . We shall send our accredited representatives to Paris, to the Peace Conference, and to the League of Nations . . ."

It was a noble and inspiring speech.

In two further public sessions the Dáil discussed the League of Nations, the Freedom of the Seas, and its social policies.

Finally, on May 9th, there was a great moment when three delegates from the Friends of Irish Freedom, in the United States were welcomed. No foreigner had addressed an Irish Parliament since Benjamin Franklin was received in the Old Irish House on College Green.

There had been raids and arrests, but in the main the British too, waited to know what would eventuate in Paris. On June 11th, President Wilson received Mr. Frank P. Walsh, the leader of the American party who had come over to help our claim. The President informed Walsh that there was an agreement among the Committee of Four (America, Britain, France and Italy) that no small nation should appear before it without the unanimous consent of the whole Committee. This meant that England could prevent Ireland from getting a hearing.

President de Valera left for America to lead the campaign there.

The Oath of Allegiance to the Irish Republic was first proposed, by the Minister for Defence, Cathal Brugha, on August 20th, 1919, the second day of the fifth session. He moved:

"Every person and every one of those bodies under-mentioned must swear allegiance to the Irish Republic and to the Dáil:

1. The Deputies.
2. The Irish Volunteers.
3. Officers and Clerks of the Dáil.
4. Any other body or individual who in the opinion of the Dáil should take the same oath".

He pointed out it was no new proceeding for a government to require that the Elected Representatives, the Defence Forces, and the Officers and Clerks of Parliament, should subscribe to an Oath of Allegiance.

He suggested an adaptation of the oath subscribed to by Congressmen, Senators and persons who aspired to become American citizens: —

"I, A.B., do solemnly swear (or affirm) that I do not and shall not yield a voluntary support to any pretended government authority, or power within Ireland, hostile and inimical thereto, and I do further swear (or affirm) that to the best of my knowledge and ability I will support and defend the Irish Republic, which is Dáil Éireann, against all enemies, foreign and domestic, and I will bear true faith and allegiance to the same, and that I take this obligation freely without any mental reservation or purpose of evasion, so help me, God". "An Oath of Allegiance was administered to every existing Government in the world . . . The present Constitution of the Irish Volunteers prevented them from being subject to any body but their own Executive. At the next Convention they proposed to ask them as a standing army to swear allegiance to the Dáil, and it was but fair and just that all members of the Dáil, should likewise subscribe to an Oath of Allegiance."

"T. MacSuibhne (Cork Mid.) seconded the motion.

"Ald. T. Kelly (St. Stephen's Green) asked if there was any necessity for this Oath . . . Was it that any of their members wished to go to the London Parliament and perform there?

"Dr. B. Cusack (Galway E.) . . . every civilised Government required an Oath of Allegiance from members of any foreign country desiring to become citizens . . . It was a perfectly just procedure.

"Mr. J. McBride (Mayo W.) was opposed to the Oath.

"Mr. W. Sears (Mayo S.) thought there was an obligation on every member to be loyal to the Republic. Even the Quakers in America took the Oath of Allegiance. As to the Volunteers, he thought it an unfortunate thing if the Dáil had no control over them.

"Liam de Roiste (Cork City) . . . the question was raised at the first session of the Dáil and members were required to sign a pledge, which he considered quite sufficient.

"Liam T. MacCosgair (Kilkenny N.) had conscientious scruples about taking an oath unless it was absolutely necessary. He would subscribe to such an Oath if adequate reasons were put forward.

"D. Kent (Cork East) it was not a question of suspicion of the trustworthiness of members that was at stake. They required to band all republicans together, and he believed that the Irish Volunteers should be under the control of the Dáil.

Arthur Griffith (Tir Eoghan and Cavan), the Acting President,

"stated that he was astonished at finding that the members had not taken an Oath of Allegiance at their first meeting. Every person elected there should pledge his or her allegiance to the standing Government of Ireland. If they were not a regular Government then they were shams and imposters. The Army and the Government of a country could not be under separate authority.

While there might be a question as to the form of the Oath there could be none as to the necessity for taking the Oath. They should realise they were the Government of the country . . . He was absolutely in favour of the motion.

"On a division 30 voted for and 15 against. The motion was carried".

In the two following sessions, those of October, 1919, and August, 1920, the Oath was administered to 53 members by the Deputy Ceann Comhairle, J. J. O'Kelly (Louth). Absent members at that time included the President, Eamon de Valera, Liam Mellows, Harry Boland, Dr. McCartan, Larry Ginnell, George Gavan Duffy, Sean T. O Ceallagh, James O'Mara, who were on official missions outside the country.

On September 11th, 1919, the British proclaimed Dáil Éireann "a dangerous association". Their plans were also maturing.

The members of the Dáil wanted to be accepted and trusted as the guardians of the nation's liberty and the people's rights, irrespective of class or politics; they wanted to preserve the unity of Ireland. Proceedings at the private session which assembled at 9.30 on Friday, 6th August, 1920 —47 members present—confronted them with an unavoidable issue.

"Sean MacEntee (Monaghan South) presented the following memorial signed by representative citizens of Belfast, which he had been asked to lay before the Dáil.

'We, the undersigned, members of the Belfast Corporation, and others, representing the views of Irish Republicans (and many others) in that city, beg to call the earnest attention of the Dáil to the war of extermination now being waged upon us, and we appeal to you to stand by us in the struggle.

We assume that you have read the press reports of the pogrom which started on July 21st with the violent expulsion from work of well over 5,000 people; of the murders, wrecking, looting and wholesale eviction of families . . .

'. . . thousands are idle here . . . The only condition on which they will be allowed to work is that they sign a declaration of loyalty to the British Government.

'We appeal to Sinn Fein, through the Dáil to take up this straight challenge, and fight Belfast—the spearhead of British power in Ireland. The Loyalists have repeatedly declared at public meetings and in the Town Council that this time they are not fighting Popery as such, but Sinn Fein, so that mere sectarianism does not enter in.

'We suggest that Sinn Fein can strike back with powerful effect by a commercial boycott of Belfast . . . The chief promoters of Orange intolerance here are the heads of the distributing trade throughout Ireland.

'. . . the most effective action (to make Belfast realise that it is in Ireland and must be of Ireland) is to . . . immediately withdraw all accounts from banks having their headquarters in Belfast . . . The above will meet with the fullest approval of nearly 100,000 people in Belfast.

'It should be strictly enjoined that Protestants in other parts of Ireland are not to be molested . . .
Signed : —Joseph Cosgrave, T.C., D. McCullough, T.C., A Savage, T.C., P.L.G., Jer Barnes, T.C., Jas. McEntee, Dr. Moore, Dr. John Doherty, Mrs. A. McCullough, P.L.G., Jas. Connolly. Dated 5th August, 1920'.

"He therefore moved . . . that an embargo be laid upon the manufacturers of the City of Belfast . . .

"Countess Markievicz : —To declare a blockade would be playing into the hands of the enemy and giving them a good excuse for Partition. It was even possible that this was a trap on the part of the English Government". She seconded Earnest Blythe's amendment to consider what action could be taken by way of a commercial embargo against individuals responsible for inciting to the recent pogroms in Belfast.

The Griffith, the Acting President, spoke, to voice his personal view: "He disagreed with the resolution and the amendment. The resolution was practically a declaration of war on one part of our own territory . . . The situation did not permit of delay. There were five or six thousand men thrown out of work, and there was no likelihood of their getting back. A printed form had been prepared which it was sought to compel every Catholic workman to sign . . . They could not stand aside. There were twelve or thirteen million pounds paid anually into Belfast banks from Leinster, Munster and Connacht . . . That could be cut off . . . It would bring the Unionist gentlemen to their senses very quickly. He would have the same objection to any other employer in any other part of Ireland imposing a test on his employees as in Belfast . . . If the Belfast employers refused to comply within seven days, then a blockade of Belfast could be declared. A white list could then be made of the firms who refuse to impose any test. Griffith's further amendment was carried: —

"That the imposition of political or religious tests as a condition of Industrial employment in Ireland is hereby declared illegal, and that action be taken by the Ministry to prevent such tests being employed in Ireland."

From this the Belfast Boycott grew. But the immediate next business of the Dáil led to the appointment of a Commission. "To Inquire into English Organised Opposition to the Republic". Its terms of reference gave it wide scope: —To devise measures for dealing with victimisation; to consider the East Ulster demand for local self-government; to ascertain how far the objections of the people of Belfast . . . to an Irish Republic may be met by a liberal scheme of devolution—based on federalised government

---

Sinn Fein propaganda in the Municipal Election campaign 1920. This was the first time for P.R. to be used nationwide. Women candidates were put forward by all parties and many of them played an important part in local administration under the first Dáil. All the cities except Belfast elected Republican Councils. The success of Sinn Fein in the election infuriated the Orange faction in Belfast.

with the county as a unit. The names of the Commission were announced at the Private Session of September 17th: Eoin MacNeill, Arthur Griffith, M. Collins, Rev. Fr. O'Kieran, Denis McCullough, Rev. Dr. Irwin, Alex MacCabe, Erskine Childers, Cathal O'Shannon, Thomas Johnson, P. MacGilligan, Desmond Fitzgerald, William Sears, Dermot Coffey, Rev. Fr. O'Flanagan, P. S. O'Hegarty, Owen O'Duffy, Sean MacEntee, J. N. Dolan, Rev. Fr. MacShane, Earnan de Blaghd, George Murnaghan, George Irvine.

Form of Ballot Paper.

Rathmines Poor Law Elections, 1920.

Your Number on the Register is..................

Your Polling Place is..

HOW TO VOTE.

Put the figure **1** in front of your favourite Candidate.
Put the figure **2** in front of your Second Choice.
Put the figure **3** in front of your Third Choice.

If you spoil a Ballot Paper ask for another.

DON'T PUT AN X ANYWHERE ON YOUR PAPER.

	Clinch, Marion.
	Cruice, Mary.
	DOYLE, CHRISTINA MARY.
	Evans, Ellen.
	Hely, Howard H.
	McCABE, WILLIAM.
	O'Connor, Elizabeth.
	PEARSE, MARGARET.

The Candidates in heavy type are the REPUBLICAN CANDIDATES. They solicit your vote and influence for that reason, and because, on principle, they will support honest, efficient administration and tolerate nothing else.

Keep this form until you have Voted, then hand it to the Sinn Fein Agent at the door of the booth.

Published by the Candidates and printed at the Powell Press, Dublin.

LABOUR'S PART

CHAPTER 5

A section of the crowds which blocked all streets leading to Mountjoy Prison when the general strike was called to force the release of hunger striking Republican prisoners.

THE day before this great issue arose so critically Dáil Éireann was recognised as the national government by an unanimous vote at the annual meeting of the Irish Labour Party and Trades Union Congress.

This brought no real change in the strength behind the Dáil because from Easter Week on the best types of men and women had rejected all middle courses and were fully prepared to stand together in total resistance to all the appeals, the demands and the threats emanating from Dublin Castle or from London.

Although the Labour movement was by no means all behind James Connolly before he died the rank and file had no difficulty in accepting his last document, which was the Proclamation of the Republic. From this moment Labour grew stronger every year, and trade unionists carried, perhaps, more than their fair share of the soldiering, with the I.R.A., and with the Citizen Army, which kept its identity. They were in the jails, among prisoners. But their greatest service was earlier in 1920 when, with the general strike, and their attendance *outside* Mountjoy Jail they not only helped powerfully to secure the release of the hunger-striking prisoners, but their adherence to the Republican side, with so much strength frightened the British Government,

A thing which Sir James MacMahon, or Sir James Taylor,[1] political civil servants in the Castle, would not have missed was that the number of delegates attending the Labour Congress had jumped to 250, from less than one hundred on every year except one, from 1896 to 1916. The report of Congress shows that it represented almost 300,000 organised workers in 1920.

In the spring of 1919, Tom Johnson and Cathal O'Shannon, the Irish Labour delegation to the International Labour and Socialist Conference at Berne, had been the first Irishmen to be accepted as representatives of their country by an international assembly following the first meeting of Dáil Éireann. On the way home they stopped in Paris to help the Dáil's official delegation to the Peace Conference.

1. Sir James Taylor. A civil servant with long experience of administering the Crimes Acts for the British Government. K.C.B. (1919). Was private secretary to Under Secretary for Ireland 1892-3; Assistant Private Secretary to Chief Secretary 1903-5; Private Secretary to Chief Secretary 1905. Chief Clerk in Chief Secretary's Office, Dublin Castle, 1911-8. Assistant Under Secretary to Lord Lieutenant, 1918. Retired 1920; sold his house, 12 Bushy Park Road. Subsequent address, 36 Old Queen Street, London (the Irish Office).

At the August Congress Tomas Cassidy explained in the course of his address that labour had not contested the 1918 election: —

> "Owing . . . to the strong desire on the part of the people that the great principle of self-determination, which was to be made the issue of the election, would not be clouded. It was this consideration only which led to the withdrawal of the Labour Party from the last General Election. If elected will Irish Labour representatives attend Westminster until such time as this country regains her freedom? . . . If we are to elect representatives we must consider the opportunity . . . to assist British Labour to mould legislation on democratic lines. We have hope in the International idea; why then should we deny our support to the champions of Labour's cause in another country when we have an opportunity of assisting them in their struggles. And it may be that the hope for Ireland's freedom will shortly rest in the hands of the democracy of Britain and the British Labour Party".

The reports of Congress in that and the following years, are indispensible reading for anyone interested in history. It should however be remembered at all times that the censorship operated, and a war was being waged outside the doors of the meeting place—no matter in which city it might be.

If one judge the importance of any event of those times by its impact on the British authorities then Limerick must take the lead in the story of Labour's contribution. But neither the Congress report on the Limerick strike, nor Dorothy Macardle's 'Irish Republic' states that the trouble arose over Robert J. Byrnes, a prominent member of the Trades and Labour Council', who was also adjutant of the 2nd Battn., Limerick Brigade, I.R.A. He was shot in his bed in the Limerick Union Hospital, by his R.I.C. guard when he was being rescued by the I.R.A.

Byrnes had been sentenced to twelve months' hard labour by a courtmartial on January 13th. He was senior officer of prisoners in the jail and led a prisoners' fight for proper conditions 'a policy of disobedience led to reprisals being taken against the prisoners. At last the prisoners rioted, led by Byrnes, wrecked the cells, smashed up the fittings . . . Their boots and clothing were removed. They were beaten up and the leaders were handcuffed day and night, put on bread and water in solitary confinement. They went on hunger strike." After three weeks Byrnes was removed to hospital in a weak condition. In the sequence of armed revolt the case of Byrnes is between Thomas Ashe—who died as a result of forcible feeding while on hunger strike in September, 1917—and Breen, Robinson and Hogan, who fired the first shots, on January 21st, 1919. The British authorities were afraid to forcibly feed again. The men who rescued Byrne should have had a car, but it was called awayt o do some urgent service for Breen and his comrades. One policeman of the hospital guard was killed —but not in time to prevent him from shooting Byrnes— and the other five were wounded.

The corpse, dressed in Michael Brennan's volunteer uniform, was symbolic of the comradeship of Pearse and Connolly two years before—almost to the date.

The report to the Irish Labour Party and Trades Union Congress—in Drogheda that August—did not put into writing the facts of the case as we know them now, and as most of those present must have known them then—ten thousand workers from Limerick being represented. I quote : —

"*Limerick Strike*: On Monday, April 14th, there began in Limerick City a strike protest against military tyranny which, because of its dramatic suddenness, its completeness, and the proof it offered that workers' control signifies perfect order, excited world attention.

"Your committee were informed by telegram that a general strike had occurred as a protest against the 'Military permit' system . . . A local volunteer had been shot . . . At the funeral British troops lined the roads with bayonets fixed, armoured cars passed the procession to and fro. Aeroplanes hovered over the hearse . . . the people declined to be provoked.

"Thereupon followed the proclamation of Limerick City as a special military area. In defining the boundaries the city was cut in two ... the effect of the proclamation was ... all workers (crossing the Shannon) had to obtain a military permit to proceed to and from their work and undergo examination at the bridge four times a day, by military sentries attended by policemen.

"With the prospect that such conditions were to come into force on the Tuesday morning hurried meetings of the Trades Council were held on Sunday ... and it was decided to call on the whole of the workers of the city to cease work on Monday morning as the most effective form of protest available to them as Trade Unionists.
"... No work was done except by permission of the Committee. Shops were allowed to open for stated periods—scales of prices were fixed—food supplies were organised ... the city was policed by the Strike patrols.
"Your committee instructed Mr. Johnson to proceed to Limerick ... to assist in every way possible the local committee.

"The National Executive ... held meetings in Limerick ... An appeal was made for funds".

The labour involvement had, in fact been started much earlier; On February 1st the Limerick Trade and Labour Council representing 35 unions, protested against the treatment of political prisoners in Limerick Jail and issued their own leaflet.

GENERAL STRIKE

LIMERICK. 1919. April

No. 286

The Workers of Limerick

Promise to Pay the bearer

10/- TEN SHILLINGS. 10/-

For the Limerick Trades and Labour Council.

Jno. Cronin ....Chairman.

J. ....Treasurer.

LIMERICK. 1919. April

AGAINST BRITISH MILITARISM.

The strike was decided upon at 11.30 p.m. on the Sunday, but by Monday morning they had a printed Proclamation displayed in the city. "There was as much 'sedition' printed in one hour during the strike as would normally get the operators ten years' imprisonment". Money was printed; also permits, lists of food prices, and a citizens' Bulletin. The Bishop of Limerick signed a manifesto, together with the principal clerics associated with his diocese. It protested not against the I.R.A., not against Labour, but against the British measures.

Numerous instances could be culled from the reports of town burnings, killings, inquests, funerals and meetings, including those of public bodies, to show labourmen active in the republican cause in their own communities. A terrifying emergency was liable to throw up the bravest on the spot civilian to take a leader's part for the time of greatest danger; he might be a rich man or a poor man, or a man self trained and experienced in trade union confrontations. The British government had proclaimed the 'national' movements, the Volunteers, Sinn Fein, Cumann na mBan, and the Fianna subversive; but even they, who were capable of almost any tyranny, did not dare to ban the trade unions—which most ministers, and certainly Sir Henry Wilson, seeing them in a wider revolutionary field, would have liked to do, in Britain as well as in Ireland.

Frank Dempsey, the railwayman who was chairman of Mallow Town Council is only one example of the local leader who stood bravely between the townspeople and the military in a gallant effort to avert the reprisal which fell on the town after Volunteers of Ernie O'Malley's command had raided the cavalry barrack and captured all the arms they were looking for. Ellen Wilkinson, the English labour leader and Dempsey were among those who gave evidence in the United States before the Commission on Conditions in Ireland.

The devoted and faithful men on the Dublin based executive seem to have been scrupulous at all times with regard to their mandate from the unions, and special conferences were held where necessary. Congress obtained their mandate from the public, too, by participating in the Local

Government elections, with their own extensive programme, for the working out of the Workers' Republic. In 120 urban districts, Labour candidates to the number of 341 secured election. 'Equally gratifying results" were obtained in the County Council, Poor Law and Rural Council elections. "Taking the local governing bodies as a whole, Labour has won a strong position", the report to the 1920 Congress states.

From the beginning Labour was represented on Dáil Committees for special purposes. It is hardly necessary to state that wage claims were not evaded when Constance Markievicz was Minister. By April, 1920, the joint implementation of the Democratic Programme and a Labour election promise led to a nation-wide control of rising food prices—following the removal by the British of restrictions imposed during the war.

When William O'Brien was arrested, the Executive wrote a vigorous letter to the British T.U.C.: —

"The only guesses we can make at a reason are: 1, That he is secretary to the Irish Labour Party and T.U. Congress, which has expressed strong views in regard to the military occupation of Ireland by foreign troops. For these views the whole Executive, indeed the whole working class movement in Ireland, are equally responsible. 2, That he is General Treasurer of . . . the I.T. & G.W.U., and has consequently engendered the dislike of the anti-labour elements who incite the Castle to action. 3, That . . . in January Mr. O'Brien was elected to the Dublin Corporation as an Alderman, after having stated in his election literature that he was in favour of establishing a Workers' Republic in Ireland".

When Labour gave its formal adherence to Dáil Éireann this was the long awaited confirmation of Connolly's great decision, which he implemented by his death in 1916. It marked the high tide of national revolution and patriotic fervour.

Yet the Congress resolution of August 5th, 1920, has to be read between the lines, and in its context, before one can describe it as I have done. The scene was in the City Hall,

Cork—soon to be burned out by the English. The Lord Mayor, Terence MacSwiney, T.D., was represented by Councillor Barry Egan; but it was Professor Alfred O'Rahilly, T.C., who explained that the Lord Mayor was attending the Oireachtas. "In that connection", Professor O'Rahilly hoped that the workers of all idealistic cognate, movements, would be working in harmony . . . The Labour movement was, perhaps, the greatest idealistic movement in Ireland at the present moment. They in Cork were idealistic, too . . . and welcomed the T.U. delegates as fellow idealists working for a common emancipation. The Labour Party relied primarily on the will of the people to produce the moral force to protest against physical compulsion . . . When they had an Irish Republic he believed Labour would not suffer for its self-sacrifice and love of moral principles; when they had a democratic Republic controlled by the Irish people, the Irish Labour Party would have the reward of having the one country in Europe with a real, genuine economic and political democracy.

Ald. E. de Roiste, T.D., Cork City:

> "The workingmen of Ireland during the past five or six years had shown that they were the only democracy in Europe that understood thoroughly what democracy was . . . They were animated by the three greatest forces on earth—the spirit of democracy, the spirit of nationality, and the spirit of true religion . . . these three forces were combined in Ireland, and they were invincible and unconquerable . . . if democratic forces did not win the alternative was the old system of militarism and capitalism, crushing the workers in all countries."

Very Rev. Dr. Thomas, O.S.F.C., Hon. President Cork and District United Trades Council:

> "Up to recent years little account was taken of such assemblies as this, because the workers were regarded as a section of the community whose interests were merely departmental . . . but the workers' attitude is the pivot on which the State revolves . . . New social conditions are bound to emerge . . . The foundations of our economic conditions are being fearlessly scrutinised, and in

certain quarters are scathingly denounced and condemned ... We are living in an atmosphere charged with momentous possibilities for the welfare or ruin of the best interests of humanity".

Terence MacSwiney, Lord Mayor, arrived late:

> "They did not recognise the conference as a mere class assembly, but as a national conference ... a bond of unity had been created amongst all Irishmen who were labouring for the welfare of an Irish Republic, and the Labour Party, generally, and representatives of Labour bodies had assisted in bringing about that bond of unity ... the operations of the army of the Republic was as much a matter for their interests as those primarily engaged in looking after the military side, for most of these men were drawn from the bodies of men the several delegates represented.

> "Ireland was carrying on a constructive movement notwithstanding what was described as a state of anarchy ... It would give their enemies much food for reflection to know that they were one for a Republic (applause) and to defend it, for they were primarily charged with the work of building up the future of Ireland".

Fifteen thousand Belfast workers were represented in Congress to be compared with 25,000 from Dublin, 10,000 each from Derry and Cork.[1]

A deputation representing the Belfast expelled workers— Messrs. Travers, O'Donovan and Hanna—was received by Congress. The full report of the discussion which took place is necessary reading, but cannot be given here. Finally Thomas Foran, Chairman:

> "It is a question of principle and not of relief. The workers of Ireland would fight to bring the issue to a

---

1. Unions represented by delegates with Belfast addresses were: N.U. of Dock and Riverside Workers; Flax Roughers and Yarn Spinners T.U. (10,000 members); Railway Clerks Assocn.; Tailors and Tailoresses U.; Tailors and Garment Workers U.; I.N.T.O.; N.U. of Tramway and Vehicle Workers; A.S. of Woodcutting Machinists; I.T. & G. W. U., Belfast Trades Council.

successful close. They had to make it clear they were not concerned with men's political or religious beliefs. They demanded the right of the Belfast Catholic or Protestant to live and work, and that he must have freedom of thought.

"Mr. Hanna had informed him that the number of persons affected is 12,000; and one fourth of them are Protestants".

He put the resolution:

"That this Congress views with regret and disgust the serious attacks made on the workers of Belfast, and authorises the incoming National Executive to take immediately whatever action they deem necessary to protect the interests of our fellow workers".

In moving the vote of thanks to the Chairman, Mr. Irvine, one of the delegates from Belfast Trades Council, said:
". . . They had their political differences in the North but were staunch under the Labour banner. In the municipal elections they carried out the contest on the straight Labour ticket and returned eleven candidates in Belfast City. These facts proved that Labour in Belfast was mindful of its duty, and did it although it was in a more difficult position than in the south. They were often told by different classes how to cure the ills existing, but he would remind those people that Labour, and Labour only will cure them, and Labour was going to do it (applause). That was the only solution. Labour will do it, and must do it".

So much for the spirit of democracy, and the spirit of nationality in Ireland at that dangerous time.

In his address to the Conference Dr. Thomas, O.S.F.C., had made the most authoritative reference to the third of the three great forces named by de Roiste, the spirit of true religion. His reference undoubtedly was to the work of the theologians—which has been buried so deep for half a century in learned journals that Pope John's pronouncements on social principles came as a surprise to the Irish public—and to the Social Action Series of Catholic Truth Society booklets, which had an immense sale.

Dáil Éireann, too, created and financed a special body to engage the best authorities they could find in the production of popular lectures—to be sold for 2d. or 3d. each. The series embraced Economics, Industrial Development, Social Problems, History, Biography, and Art. About one quarter of the 44 titles was published before the end of the period of glory.

This whole section of literature calls for the attention of all those people living to-day who wish to be informed about the nature of the development in Irish government which was planned by the successors of the men who died in Easter Week.

The printers and publishers and distributors of Irish revolutionary material deserve mention here because they supplied the very eager demand of the young for more and more reading matter. Tone, Emmet, O'Connell, the Young Irelanders, Michael Davitt were in paper cover editions long before 1916. To these (and others) Fintan Lalor was added; and Willie Rooney; then came Connolly and Pearse and the Resurrection of Hungary. 1916 produced its own literature. To a library on Ireland already assembled in rich and varied profusion—including Hyde, Yeats, Green, Stephens—was added such pamphlets as "The Ethics of Sinn Fein", Robert Lynd, and an avalanche of ballads and politics. The great documents of Dáil Éireann were generally available—particularly the fine printing to which Fergus O'Connor defiantly attached his name as publisher. Terence MacSwiney, dying on hunger strike, left as his major legacy, "The Principles of Freedom".

No one should think himself informed on this period of Irish history who knows only about its battles, and its attitude to the English aggression. Worthy though these are of the fullest understanding, there are other voices which deserve hearing:

Rev. W. P. Hackett, S.J., on Municipal government:

"If we have our young citizens abounding in civic sense they will take their part in these bodies . . ."

On corruption in public affairs:

"To use a trust position as a means of giving a job

would be to act like the doctor who felt your pulse and filched your watch".

On the Popular Lecture series:

"The whole idea is to try and diffuse knowledge and culture over every part of Ireland. The moment is propitious. There is a vast enthusiasm. If this is properly canalised the nation will become an oasis of knowledge and culture . . .

"The new soul that has come into Ireland is strong as well as young. If its strength is guided in the proper manner it will be trained to consider others. Looking back on the splendid achievements of Christianity in the Golden Age, when sectarianism did not tamper with the work of Christ, it will brace itself to new efforts to produce a state where crime may be less, comfort may be more, and where virtue may abound".

Rev. L. McKenna, S.J., on the Social Teachings of James Connolly:

"An examination of these writings seems to impose irresistably the conclusion that Connolly's deepest, strongest passion was his love of Ireland . . . his socialism, though sincere and enthusiastic, was primarily adopted because it seemed to promise . . . a free and prosperous Irish people . . . Connolly's voice is the voice of Tone or Fintan Lalor, though his words are often the words of Marx . . . He was very original in his thinking. His socialism was not a copy but an adaptation".

Alfred O'Rahilly, writing on "Some Theology about Tyranny"—Irish Theological Quarterly, Oct., 1920, was then a military prisoner. The fact that the censor acted to prevent him from checking his sources, with the help of English friends, perhaps accounts for his choice of title.

Rev. Dr. S. Ceileachair, D.D., on Labour:

"However much Labour may seem to have advanced it certainly cannot be said to be at the expense of capital, for while it may be able to raise wages it has not yet shown any signs of being able to reduce profits. And the mighty chasm which separates the wealthy capitalist from humble worker remains as formally set as ever".

On Arbitration Boards:

"Let it be made unmistakably clear that such arbitration boards as I am pleading for can be relied upon to give all in the country a fair opportunity of sharing in . . . industries, and labour will soon come in to support them, and abide by their decision . . . Let Labour be over represented in them, since to Labour is due exceptional guarantees of fair play . . . Let them be convinced that a movement is on foot for the advantage of Ireland as a whole in which they can participate on terms of equality with all others, and they will not be backward in taking a patriotic and constructive part". *Dail Lecture Series.*

Rev. P. Coffey, Ph.D., Maynooth:

"How is the Irish State to set about making the sources of Irish wealth—agricultural, industrial and commercial —subserve the well being of the Irish nation? . . . The Catholic Doctrine of Property . . . Private Ownership: duties and obligations. The Capitalist State; necessity to reform". (Headings taken from a Catholic Truth Society booklet, 1920.)

These were some of the signs indicating that powerful forces within the Irish Revolution would, if allowed, implement Christian ideals in the formation of the system of government under the Irish Republic being developed under the first Dáil Éireann.

It was clear to the English planners of Home Rule for Ireland that a Communist Plot was the thing to try. If that could be put forward convincingly the Irish side could be split. Reading descriptions of the hymn-singing crowds outside Mountjoy Jail, when Labour declared a general strike in support of hunger-striking republican prisoners, the plotters in Dublin Castle and/or Whitehall, or Unionist Headquarters, Grafton Street, decided that the plot, at least in its early stages, should be whispered only, in Ireland.

By January, 1920, the British government was in more trouble than Dáil Éireann. Churchill announced to the Commons that 43,000 troops were in Ireland. British Labour sent a delegation of inquiry, to find out the truth of what was happening. Lord French, in an interview said that order would be restored if martial law was proclaimed but this would be done only as a last resort. It was done, presently and, as well as that, the Black and Tans made their first appearance on March 25th. They were followed by the "Gentleman's Corps", the auxiliaries.

In the first local government election Sinn Fein and Republican Labour won all the cities and boroughs except Belfast; by June they had the counties also. Alderman Tom Kelly, T.D., became Lord Mayor of Dublin—but he was in Gloucester Jail and meanwhile gallant Larry O'Neill carried on.

The Roman Catholic Hierarchy, meeting in Maynooth: "The legitimate demand of Ireland...to choose her own government has not only been denied her, but every organ for the expression of her national life has been ruthlessly suppressed and her people subjected to an iron rule of oppression as cruel and unjust as it is ill-advised and out of date".

King George, addressing the British Parliament, was (despite the terms of his Coronation Oath) 'concerned' about Ireland—as well he might be considering promises and pledges dishonoured, and the slaughter done in his name—"A Bill will immediately be laid before you to give effect to the proposals for the better government of *that country*".

This heralded the Partition Bill—foulest blow of all—to which was added after a few weeks, an oath of allegiance.

"A mockery", the Archbishop of Cashel called it, on March 3rd.

But by St. Patrick's Day, the U.S. Senate reaffirmed its sympathy with the Irish People and hoped "that the time is at hand when Ireland will have a government of her own choosing".

Next day, March 18th, Thomas MacCurtin, the Lord Mayor of Cork, was shot. The inquest jury returned a verdict of "Wilful Murder" against the English Prime Minister, the Viceroy and the Chief Secretary as well as against three Inspectors of the R.I.C. and members of the force. Lord French and Sir James Taylor, who had seemed to speak with some knowledge about the murder, were invited to give evidence at this inquest; neither came.

Terence MacSwiney, T.D., succeeded Thomas MacCurtin as Lord Mayor of Cork. Although a Volunteer officer he tried to stand his ground and perform his municipal duties; but he was arrested in the City Hall on August 11th and died on hunger strike in Brixton Prison, London, in October.

In his inaugural speech MacSwiney spoke for all of us who were endeavouring to make government work:

> "We see in the manner in which the late Lord Mayor was murdered an attempt to terrify us all. Our first duty is to answer that threat in the most fitting manner: to show ourselves unterrified, cool and inflexible for the fulfilment of our chief purpose—the establishment of the independence and the integrity of our country and the peace and happiness of the Irish Republic. To that end I am here.

> "It is not those who inflict the most, but those that can suffer the most who will conquer, though we do not abrogate our function to demand that murderers and evil doers be punished for their crimes. Those whose faith is strong will endure to the end in triumph".

Matters to which reference is not to be found in the published reports of Dáil Éireann include President de Valera's interview with the Westminster Gazette, February 6th, 1920, and the Partition of Ireland, which was accomplished by the English, using military force to establish the Border, during the lifetime of the first Dáil, in 1921.

While Terence MacSwiney had no more conception of what would happen after his death than the majority of his colleagues in republican politics, or his comrades in the Republican Army—giving their lives daily—he must have known and discussed de Valera's interview and its implications. Yet a man of his calibre and integrity could die himself, under dreadful circumstances, and call on others to suffer whatever was necessary! We do not know whether he knew that the Dáil Cabinet had divided on this issue. I can do no more than draw the attention of students—who sooner or later must get access to the facts—to the obscurities which confound me!

I have already quoted enough to establish that Freedom of the Seas was a question of major principle in the early official documents of Dáil Éireann. One must ask how that was affected, if at all, by the President's statement:

> "The United States by the Monroe Doctrine made provision for its security without depriving the Latin Republics of the South of their independence and their life. The United States safeguarded itself from the possible use of the island of Cuba as a base for an attack by a foreign power by stipulating: 'That the government of Cuba shall never enter into any treaty or other compact with any foreign Power or Powers which will impair or tend to impair the independence of Cuba, nor in any manner authorise or permit any foreign Power or Powers to obtain, by colonisation, or for military or naval purposes or otherwise, lodgement in or control over any portion of said island'.

> "Why doesn't Britain make a stipulation like this to safeguard herself against foreign attack as the United States did with Cuba? Why doesn't Britain declare a Monroe Doctrine for the two neighbouring islands? The people of Ireland so far from objecting would co-operate with their whole soul".

Dr. Patrick McCartan, T.D., Liam Mellows, T.D., Harry Boland, T.D., and James O'Mara, T.D., were with de Valera in the States at the time; "He had consulted none of us. We had no hint he was about to issue a statement. It came as a thunderbolt to us", wrote Dr. McCartan. "de Valera opens the Door", wrote The Globe. "This statement is a withdrawal by the official head of the Irish Republic of the demand that Ireland be set free to decide her own international relations".

McCartan wondered "Was he carrying out the secret policy of the Cabinet in telling England that though he was going up and down the United States as President of the Republic, Ireland would be content to accept the status of a vassal Republic like Cuba in order to safeguard England's security?"

McCartan was sent back to Dublin by the President, to explain, and he attended a cabinet meeting:

"I gave de Valera's explanation, which was substantially as follows: First, he had wanted to start England talking so that some basis of settlement might be considered; secondly he quoted only one paragraph of the Platt Amendment relating to Cuba, to show that Ireland was willing to discuss safeguards for English security compatible with Ireland's independence; and lastly that only his enemies had put a hostile interpretation on the interview.

"Countess Markievicz commented that de Valera talked only for himself and could not commit the Dáil even if he wanted to. Count Plunkett and Cathal Brugha showed marked hostility to the proposal and desired to discuss it separately. But Collins and Griffith shut down the discussion".

My own memory of the republican reaction to the Cuba interview was that we were extremely uneasy about it, but prepared to admit we had no sinister motives against England, should we win our freedom we would not attack or invade her! Perhaps it was no harm to let that be known in advance.

Arthur Griffith's last occasion to be Acting President at a Dáil meeting was on September 17th, 1920. Forty six members attended. By that time Republican Courts and the Republican police were well established. Most public bodies had given allegiance to Dáil Éireann. Enemy police barracks and income tax offices had been burned in large numbers. Some of the more well off citizens of the Republic were paying income tax to Dáil Éireann—people like the Daly's of Limerick. Ministers in prison included Robert Barton, Desmond Fitzgerald; backbenchers Terence MacSwiney, and I do not know who else.

Griffith reported that some leaders of the Irish Unionist Party had

> "recently visited him and asked if peace could not be arranged. They asked if he would submit proposals from them to Dáil Éireann. He told them that Dáil Éireann would receive proposals from any body of Irishment, and would send a courteous reply. They subsequently submitted a scheme for the establishment of a Commonwealth connected with England. These proposals were placed before the Ministry who decided that they contained no basis for a settlement. He suggested that counter proposals would be sent to the Unionists and they be asked what guarantees they would require from the Republic. They should be met by the Commission on Organised Resistance to the Republic which was being set up".

The Dáil worked hard from 9.15 a.m. to 7 p.m. It took reports from the Ministries of Propaganda, Home Affairs, Foreign Affairs, Finance, Labour, Local Government, Industry and Commerce, Agriculture, Fisheries and Defence. It ratified an Assistant Minister for Irish and discussed the appointment of a town clerk in Waterford. Towards the end of the day it voted £400 for the Commission on Organised Opposition to the Republic, settled its terms of reference, and appointed Eoin MacNeill, Arthur Griffith, M. Collins, Rev. Fr. O'Kieran, Denis MacCullough, Rev. Dr. Irwin, Alec McCabe, Erskine Childers, Cathal O'Shannon, Thomas Johnston, P. MacGulligan, Desmond Fitzgerald, William Sears, Dermot Coffey, Rev. Fr. O'Flanagan, P. S. O'Hegarty, Owen O'Duffy, Sean MacEntee, J. N. Dolan, Rev. Fr. MacShane, Earnan de Blaghd, George Irvine and George Murnaghan to be members of the Commission.

The Dáil passed a Decree for the Protection of Irish Industries, a Bill for the formation of an Economic Council, and a Bill for the establishment of the National Land Commission.

The Acting President read from the Irish Independent that an American Commission on British Atrocities in Ireland was being set up.

Arthur Griffith was arrested before there could be another meeting that Session. Michael Collins became Acting President and during his period there does not appear to have been any meeting of the Dáil.

The 1921 Session opened on Dáil Éireann's second birthday 21st January, 1921, with twenty four members attending. "The Deputy Speaker said that the President found it necessary to alter his plans and he could not be present. The President arrived at that decision in consultation with the Ministers of Finance and Defence. Some reports were read (unspecified). Finally a resolution was proposed by Liam de Roiste, and seconded by R. M. Sweetman:

"That this Session of Dáil now adjourn owing to its inability to discuss adequately important questions of policy in the unavoidable absence of responsible Ministers, and we request the President to have a statement ready to be submitted to the Dáil so that definite decisions on policy can be come to by the Dáil. A meeting of the Dáil to be held, if possible at once".

The Session adjourned. Members in prison included Griffith, Markievicz, MacNeill, Staines, Barton, Duggan, Fitzgerald and more.

On January 25th R. M. Sweetman put his point that the shooting of the enemy secret service men on 'Bloody Sunday' had been a mistake. "He was in total disagreement with the policy pursued for some time back . . . They were absolutely presenting the enemy with the solution he wanted . . . He refused to be put down as a pacifist but he wanted to see nothing done which they, as moderate men, could not standover . . . He thought it absolutely necessary to call off the form of activity which culminated in the events of that Sunday. In his letter to the press he had proposed a conference of certain public bodies, not for the purpose of negotiating but of suggesting a preliminary truce to peace. He considered that such a course would have been better than to follow the pourparlers that did take place. His letter was sent before the arrest of Griffith and MacNeill. If he had committed an indiscretion it was due to the fact that, as a member of the Dáil, he had not been put in possession of essential facts. There was some controversy and members, while disagreeing, upheld Sweetman's rights to his views.

Kevin O'Higgins, Assistant Minister for Local Government, praised the members from Cork, and North Wexford, de Roiste and Sweetman, for their moral courage, but said they made a mistake in considering merely the results of the moment:

"If a lorry load of Black and Tans were ambushed, and a large area burned as a reprisal they merely set one fact against the other and said the odds were with the enemy. They did not take into account that while England got £50,000,000 out of Ireland, the Administration of this country was costing her £100,000,000. They did not at all weigh the effect of the reprisal campaign on Labour and Liberals ... They merely look at Ireland and seem to forget the fight going on in India, Egypt and South Africa ... Their statements ... did not reflect the views of their constituents or the country as a whole. He considered any slackening of military activities would be a mistake and would convince the English that the republicans were on the run.

Sean MacEntee said he had urged the necessity for frequent Dáil meetings. The Ministry did not seem to pay any attention to his arguments ... they were of the opinion that they could govern the country while the Dáil was in a state of hibernation ... Many members ... had no means of keeping in touch. He hoped it would be the policy of the Ministry to bring the Dáil together more frequently. He thought they should be as tenacious as possible. They should attack the British military forces in the North.

Michael Collins defended the Ministry and described the negotiations initiated by Lloyd George through Archbishop Clune. Austin Stack, Richard Mulcahy, M. P. Colivet, P. O'Keeffe, Liam de Roiste, P. Beaslai all took part in a most important discussion in which they gave their straight opinions on the state of the defence of the country. The President listened to their views. Invited to speak, he discussed the feasibility of accepting a formal state of war,

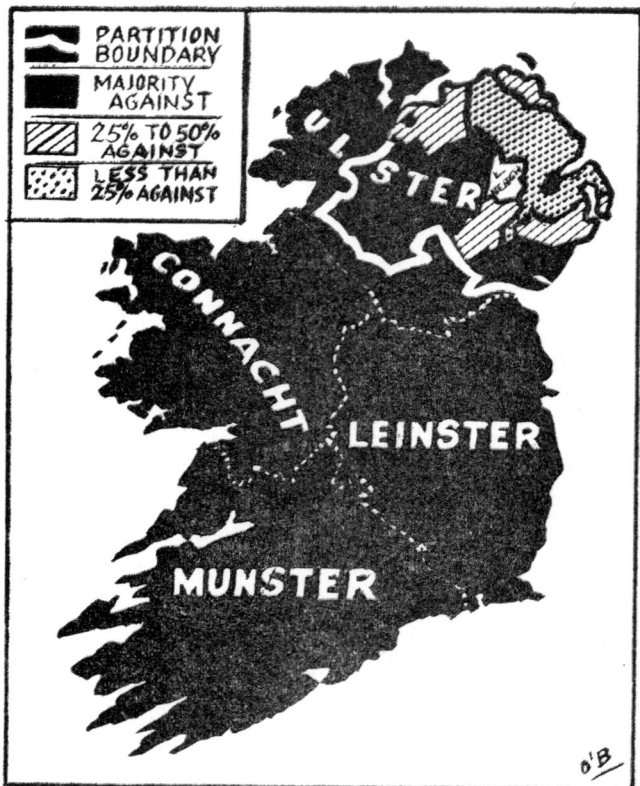

Early in 1921 the cruel line which no Irishman had voted for was pushed across Ireland by military force under the British Government of Ireland Act. The County Councils of Tyrone and Fermanagh and the Local Government unions of Crossmaglen, Cookstown, Dungannon, Enniskillen, Irwinstown, Kilkeel, Lisnaskeagh, Magherafelt, Newry, Omagh and Strabane representing a little over half the total partitioned area, at that time had Nationalist majorities— Parliamentary representatives of Derry, Tyrone and Fermanagh sat in the first Dáil, while Armagh and Down, represented by Michael Collins and Eamon de Valera, joined with the others in the second Dáil.

which was being thrust on them: —

> "Members who did not agree with the policy should ask what was the alternative. If they were to cease volunteer activities could they carry on peacefully? They could not. Could they carry on constructive work? They could not. The enemy would force them out of pacifism by brutality . . . So far from being a vote of censure on the Ministry the sense of the meeting was an endorsement of their action".

De Valera reported on his mission to U.S.A.—without reference to Cuba—and departmental reports were taken in the normal way. Estimates for the half year ending June, 1921, were approved. They amounted to £185,900. The whole of Munster, from Wexford and Kilkenny were under martial law since the New Year and Dublin came under Curfew in February. Michael Colivet, T.D., Limerick, was carried as a hostage in a military lorry—a thing that happened all the time to civilians, as important as H.M. Forces could apprehend from among known Republicans. On March 7th, three days before the next Dáil Session, George Clancy, newly elected Mayor of Limerick, completed his official business concerning the Dáil Loan, with Daithi O Donnachadha, Secretary to the Trustees of Dáil Éireann. As Daithi left Clancy's house, a military pandemonium broke out in the city. He had to run, and hide, and crawl by turn before he could get back to his hotel: his attache case was full of money received and checked with Clancy. Next morning in the train to Dublin he read of the murders of Clancy and ex-Lord Mayor Michael O'Callaghan and Volunteer Joe O'Donogue by Auxiliaries the night before. The train was searched for Daithi but he was safe enough in his first class carriage, smoking a cigar and reading his paper with apparent unconcern. The people gave a lot of money—by revolutionary standards. Keeping it safely was Daithi's job.

The British counter attack—subject for a separate study—was then running strongly. It can be dissected now that one is almost fifty years older and can at leisure set out its shape and strength under suitable headings for the judgment of history. In the present volume I am concerned with the members of Dáil Éireann, who were human flesh and blood, brave and puzzled, trying to battle through. We are looking at men who in some cases were entering the last stages of a great, inspired comradeship. It even remains to be discovered whether we have or have not a fair *official* report of what happened. Certainly we were allowed to have no proper accounts in the Irish newspapers. Most of them had been through a long period of total suppression because they had published paid advertisements for the Dáil Éireann Loan.

The British Press censorship operated with great subtlety. Because a constant stream of foreign journalists was following all surface events, and were sending first hand reports in many directions the accounts of ambushes, town burnings, destruction of co-operative creameries, Crown Force murders and local inquests could not be withheld from the Irish papers, although such reports were submitted to censor daily. But how much can one find now about the driving of the Border from the Irish Sea to Lough Swilly by a military force.

We laughed hard at the thought that the English could make a lasting partition of Ireland against the practically unanimous will of the Irish people. Alas we had no conception either of their great ability, or the depths to which they would descend when the Conference stage would be reached, their smile and their handshake more deadly than war.

Dáil Éireann carried on its own world, quite ignorant of what its leaders were doing, striving to make Government function; and there was no mention of Partition until Piarais Beaslai brought up the elections, which the British had proclaimed for the Twenty Six Counties—"Southern Ireland"—and the Six Counties—"Northern Ireland. This was on March 11th. We are not given the Report of the Department of Home Affairs, but only a section of the debate on it.

P. Beaslai "considered the statement that the Ministry had decided to contest the elections for the Ulster Parliament very important. He was surprised that it was not put down on the agenda for discussion, and he thought it was a matter which should be discussed on the report. Most of them had no opportunity of discussing or considering it ... He thought the subject should not be passed without full consideration. He was in favour of a contest, but it had been suggested that the effect of a contest would be to consolidate a solid Orange Block".

The President said to a large extent *it was a matter for the Sinn Fein Executive. The aspect which came before the Dáil was the acceptance of a foreign law arranged by a foreign Government. The whole matter had been gone into by Sinn Fein and by the Ministry and they had decided in favour of a contest ...*
The President then detailed the negotiations which had taken place between the Republican Party and Mr. Devlin ... the basis of the agreement would be abstention.

Sean MacEntee (Monaghan South) said that "this question concerned not only Ulster but the whole of Ireland ... The question of contesting the elections was not one for Sinn Fein, but for the Dáil, since it was the authority of the Dáil which was challenged".

The report was adopted.

As always they had a full reading of Ministerial reports and passed a decree to exclude English goods and added one more to the decrees regulating rent increases. The Substitute Director of Agriculture introduced his Land Scheme to relieve unemployment in agriculture.

The President proposed the formal acceptance of a state of war with England. This was agreed to unanimously.
On May 3rd President de Valera issued an address to the Electroate:

"Dáil Éireann, the elected Government of Ireland, has given its sanction to the Parliamentary elections now pending in order that you may have an opportunity of proving once more your loyalty to the principle of Irish Independence ...
"You who vote for Sinn Fein candidates will cast your votes for nothing less than the legitimacy of the Repub-

lic, for Ireland against England, for freedom against slavery, for right and justice against force and wrong, here and everywhere . . .

"The issue between Ireland and England will never be settled until it is settled on the basis of right. We are advancing steadily to that settlement. The blossoms are not the fruit but the precursors of the fruit—beware how you pluck them".

If fine words could have won the Irish Republic, he might have led us to it.

At the final session of the First Dáil, on May 10th, he moved:

1. That the Parliamentary elections which are to take place during the present month be regarded as elections to Dáil Éireann.

The Custom House.
British departments of government burned out of it by Irish Government forces on May 25th included the local government Board, Excise and Customs, Stamps and Taxes, Stationery Office. The staffs operated subsequently from Jurys Hotel, the Presbyterian Hall, Abbey Street, the Four Courts and St. John's Road, Kingsbridge.

2. That all members duly returned at these elections be regarded as members of Dáil Éireann and allowed to take their seats on subscribing to the proposed Oath of Allegiance to the Republic.

3. That the present Dáil dissolve automatically as soon as the new body has been summoned by the President and called to order.

4. That the Ministry remain in power until the new Dáil has met and will thereupon resign their portfolios through the President.

In reply to a question the President said that everyone elected to the Northern or Southern Parliament was entitled to be summoned, Unionists and all.

The President said they had now come to the point where they felt they had turned the corner.

Nevertheless, there was a feeling that meetings, from then on would be more difficult to hold. At the previous session the acting speaker had then taken the sense of the House on the proposal that the Dail should continue to function until its membership was reduced to five and that it should then resolve itself into a Provisional Government.

At Easter—which in 1921 fell on March 27th—the Labour Party and Trades Union Congress issued an appeal to the nation generally, and to its government in which they asked that the burdens resulting from the great world war, and our own war of liberation, would be shared as equally as possible among all classes in the Irish community. They spoke for 110,000 persons unemployed out of a total labour force in the whole country of about 700,000.

This document quoted the Democratic Programme, and it acknowledged that some of the reforms requested had already been legislated by Dáil Éireann.

The Labour proposals were *not* a demand for worker control of industry but the document stated

"the enfranchisement of the working class industrially will be easier if the problems of economic production and equitable distribution are dealt with on these lines".

The proposals "provide a means of saving our country from imminent economic destruction at the hands of external force".

Enough food was produced to feed everybody . . .
"If people have food and if their labour is directed towards providing the other necessaries and comforts of life we shall suffer neither unemployment nor destitution . . . A moratorium should be announced suspending the payment of rents and land purchase annuities 'for the duration of the war'."

A reorganisation of the country's agricultural, industrial and financial systems was called for. Farmers of 20 acres or more were asked to give a voluntary tithe of their holdings on which labourers, donating overtime work, would produce food "to be devoted directly to the national service". Industrialists were asked to sacrifice their profits, but to keep the machine going; local bodies and traders were called upon to buy Irish and the consuming public in the national interest to make sacrifices corresponding to those being made by the people generally in the national cause. The document is evidence of the high spirit of idealism which existed at that time, and its perusal is necessary to any studenty who wishes to understand the complexities and the rivalries which developed in the life span of the Second Dáil.

The Manifesto was signed by Thomas Foran, and Thomas Johnson and it concluded:

"For our part, we insist that while Ireland's industries must be encouraged, protected and developed, the purpose of it all must be kept clearly in mind, dominating all our thoughts, inspiring all our activities, that purpose being to build a nation which shall be the master, not the slave, of its material wealth, a nation of free and fearless, healthy, happy and noble men and women".

The Dáil report of the meeting of May 10th contains no indication that Labour's Manifesto was raised; but in the absence of full information, and reassurance concerning the validity of the official reports, it is impossible to be sure that it was not raised.

At the end of this last Session of the First Dáil Éireann one can imagine the members, and the ministers, leaving their secret meeting place in ones and twos, walking or cycling into the rush hour traffic in streets where murder always walked.

Three days later was nomination day when, apart from a few who retired, they were re-elected—together with new-comers. In the result 124 were returned unopposed, with a mandate to support Dáil Éireann. A further six, with the same mandate, were successful in contested elections in Derry, Tyrone-Fermanagh, Armagh, and Down.[1]

A further stimulating feature of this election was that Eamon de Valera, President of the Republic was returned for County Down, and the Minister for Finance, Michael Collins for County Armagh—both, of course, in the area severed from the rest of Ireland by England's Border. Griffith already had his seat in Tyrone-Fermanagh. We, rank and file Republicans, got the impression that our leaders were standing in person to defend the Thirty Two County Republic at the point of greatest danger.[2]

1.   In the way the issue in this election was presented in the British Act of Parliament the Irish people were asked to vote in favour of the partition of their country into two statelets both swearing allegiance to King George, and having very limited powers within the Empire. The alternative was Crown Colony Government—so the English had it both ways.

2.   Nevertheless it is clear now that the partnership of Pearse and Connolly had broken down, and worse again, that counter revo-lution was running strongly, with the Republican leadership in-volved. It had been arranged that the cabinet of the First Dáil would remain in charge until it handed over to the Second Dáil; the changeover was in the hands of the President. But no Dáil was summoned until August 17th. I am assuming here that the Truce, July 11th, and the events before and after it, were beyond the power of the First Dáil either to ratify or condemn. The old cabinet had decided that there would be no meeting with the British in London. The proper place to meet them would be a neutral country, or on the ship of such a country. Even Lloyd George had agreed with Patrick Moylet, Griffith's agent, that London would not be a suitable place. Yet London it was!

Letter from the late Sean T. O Ceallaigh

UACHTARAN NA hÉIREANN

Baile Átha Cliath,
9 Samhain, 1946.

Miss Maire Comerford,
St. Nessan, Sandford, Co. Dublin.

A Chara,

It is good to know the "civil aspect of the Republican Government 1919-'21" is to receive attention . . .
It would give me great pleasure to assist you in this commendable effort . . .

It is not correct that I presided at the first or any meet-
—ings of the Cabinet of the Republican Government. Neither was I a member of the Cabinet. I was privileged to be present at a short meeting of the Cabinet which was held at the Mansion House immediately after the first public meeting of Dáil Éireann on Monday, January 21st. As far as my recollection goes, all that happened at that meeting was to arrange for a time and place of meeting for the Cabinet for the following day.

By invitation of the Cathaoirleach, Cathal Brugha, I was present for a time at the Cabinet meeting held on January 22nd, at the Mansion House. It was at that meeting I was nominated to be a speaker of Dáil Éireann, which nomination was later confirmed by the Dáil. It was at that meeting also that sanction was given to the proposition already made by the Foreign Affairs Committee of Sinn Fein that I should be sent to Paris to endeavour to get from the Peace Conference about to open there a hearing for the delegates later appointed by Dáil Éireann to present Ireland's case to the Peace Conference.

Another reason why I was asked to attend the first two meetings of the Cabinet of the Government of the Irish Republic was because I had been largely responsible for the details of all the arrangements made for the calling of the Dáil into existence.

The responsibility for the arrangements for the assembly of the Dáil were placed by those who were elected to the Dáil on the Standing Committee of Sinn Fein. The elected persons met in the Mansion House on either January 7th or 8th—I am not certain which day—and decided that the Dáil would be called together as the Parliament of the Republic of Ireland. That body also decided, on my proposition, that all the elected representatives, to whatever party they belong, should be invited to attend that meeting. I was appointed by the Sinn Fein Standing Committee chairman of a sub-commitee to make the arrangements. I do not now remember accurately the names of all the members of this sub-committee, but it is certain that the following were members:
Rev. M. O Flannagain, acting President of Sinn Fein as ex-officio member;
Harry Boland;
Seoirse Gavan Duffy, and
J. J. Walshe.

There were some others but I do not now recollect who they were.

I did have a considerable number of papers and documents relating to these meetings, but when I was arrested during the Civil War, in June, 1922, all my papers were taken away by the C.I.D. and I was afterwards told that they had been burned.

... I will do all I can to assist you in the work you have undertaken. I think, however, that it is probable that Mr. Gavan Duffy, now President of the High Court would be in a position to be much more helpful with regard to this period of our history. My recollection is that he acted in the beginning as Secretary of the Cabinet, before Diarmuid O'Hegarty was brought in ... I left Dublin for Paris the first days of February, 1919.

Yours sincerely,

Sean T. O Ceallaigh.

AN ARD-CHUIRT BREITHEAMHNAIS
(High Court of Justice)

Na Ceithre Cuirteanba
(Four Courts)

BAILE ÁTHA CLIATH

November 13th, 1946.

Dear Miss Comerford,

In reply to your letter, I was Secretary to the Dáil for some four months in 1918-19 until I went to Paris as Envoy; after that Diarmuid O'Hegarty acted and he has far more information than I. If you like I could look up old files to see if there are any records of the early days, but I should have to postpone this till the Christmas holidays, as it takes time and I am working under great pressure during the term.

Yours sincerely,

George Gavan Duffy.

BRITISH GOVERNMENT IN IRELAND, 1915.

Changes affecting the estates and sources of wealth of the landlord class in Ireland did not make any difference to their role in national or local administration under the Viceroy. The following extract from Thom's Directory, 1915 (reprinted by kind pemrission of the owners, Messrs. Hely Thom) shows the structure of British Government in Ireland the year before the Rising.

The Executive Government is vested in a Viceroy, assisted by a Privy Council appointed by the Crown ... The Lord Lieutenant is also assisted by a Chief Secretary, who is a member of the House of Commons.

Each County is in charge of a Lieutenant, generally a peer, an indefinite number of Deputy Lieutenants and Magistrates, who act gratuitously, and one or more Resident paid Magistrates, all appointed by the Crown during pleasure.

The country is represented in the Imperial Parliament by 28 Temporal Peers and 103 Commons . . . The electors on the register in 1914 numbered 698,098 persons. *Military Divisions.* The staff of Ireland consists of Commander of the Forces, Adjutant General, and Quartermaster General, Three Military Districts : — Dublin, Cork, Belfast . . . *The Militia of Ireland* . . . is now included in the Special Reserve of the British Army . . . Of the 55,606 non-commissioned officers and men of the Special reserve on 1st October, 1913, 12.462 were born in Ireland.

The Royal Irish Constabulary and Dublin Metropolitan Police : The Constabulary forces on 30th Sept., 1913 . . . consisted of an Inspector General, 1 Deputy Inspector General, 2 Assistant Inspector Generals . . . 36 County Inspectors, 197 District Inspectors, 236 Head Constables, 1,675 Sergeants, 369 Acting Sergeants, and 8,021 Constables—total 10,544".

"Effective strength per 10,000 of the population gives us the following order in counties and Cities : —Galway 49; Clare 46; Tipperary N.R. 33; Belfast 32; Westmeath 35; Roscommon and Waterford, Kings County 30; Kilkenny, Limerick 28; Dublin, Meath, Sligo, Tipperary S.R. 27; Leitrim, Longford, Londonderry 26; Wicklow, Waterford 25; Queen's 23; Carlow, Cork E.R., Cork City, Limerick City 22; Fermanagh, Kerry, Kildare, Mayo, 21; Cork W.R., Donegal 20; Louth 19; Wexford 18; Tyrone, Cavan 17; Armagh, Monaghan 16; Antrim 14; Down, Londonderry County 13."

All Judges were appointed. Everybody in above lists was appointed.

No elected body higher than county council or corporation existed in Ireland. No elected person, except the Lord Mayor of Dublin—and he only within the city, by definition *not* in the Viceregal Lodge—had any place at all in the Roll of Precedence in Ireland.

The Crown had the free services of 2,700 Lieutenants and Deputy Lieutenants of Counties and Magistrates.

Its paid heads of departments and officers of government numbered about 2,000.

George V was the 38th King of England from "The Conquest".

There had been 115 Viceroyalties since 1361.

Mr. Augustine Birrell was the 55th Chief Secretary since 1802—when the Act of Union was carried under circumstances which are notorious.

SINN FEIN ASKS SOME QUESTIONS

Ireland was a wealthy country which England was running at a profit.

Sinn Fein asked the question: — "Are we alone among the nations created to be slaves and helots ... Did God Almighty set up this island to be a sandbank for England to walk on? Is it the sole mission of Irish men and women to send beef and butter to John Bull?

"Are we too small in area? We are double Switzerland or Denmark, nearly three times Holland or Belgium. Is our population too small—though it was once double? We are as numerous as Serbia, our population is as large as that of Switzerland and nearly double that of Denmark or Norway. Does the difficulty lie in our poverty? The revenue raised per head in Ireland is double that of any other small nation ... The total revenue of Ireland is ten times that of Switzerland, three times that of Norway, four times that of Denmark, Serbia or Finland. Yet all these countries have their own armies ... They run themselves as free nations far below the cost of servile Ireland. Why? Because there is no other country pocketing their cash.

Her are some figures: —

	Area (thousands of sq miles)	Population (millions)	Revenue (Millions £s.)
Ireland	32½	4½	30
Belgium	11½	7½	32
Holland	12½	6½	18¾
Denmark	15½	2¾	7½
Norway	125	2½	10
Switzerland	16	4	3
Rumania	53½	7½	24
Serbia	34	4½	8½
Finland	126	3¼	8½

"These figures would suggest that Ireland is a strong military and naval power among the small nations. And so we are—only the army and navy we support are not our own.

"It is about time we started business on our own."
("The Issue"—the case for Sinn Fein by Lector. As passed by censor. New Ireland Publishing Company Ltd., 13 Fleet St., Dublin, 1918.)

Archbishop's House,
Dublin.
8th May, 1917.

Dear Sir,

The question may perhaps be asked, why a number of us, Irish Bishops, Catholic and Protestant, have thought it worth our while to sign a protest against the partitioning of Ireland. Has not that miserable policy, condemned as it has been by the all but unanimous voice of Nationalist Ireland, been removed, months ago, from the sphere of practical politics?

Nothing of the kind. Anyone who thinks that partition, whether in its naked deformity, or under the transparent mask of "county option", does not hold a leading place in the practical politics of to-day, is simply living in a fool's paradise.

Faithfully yours,

William J. Walsh,

Archbishop of Dublin.

[For "Edition Evening Herald"]

Dear Sir,

The question may perhaps be asked, why a number of us, Irish Bishops, Catholic and Protestant, have thought it worth our while to sign a protest against the partitioning of Ireland. Has not that miserable policy, condemned as it has been by the all but unanimous voice of Nationalist Ireland, been removed, months ago, from the sphere of practical politics?

Nothing of the kind. Any one who thinks that partition, whether in its naked deformity, or under the transparent mask of "county option" does not hold a leading place in the practical politics of to-day, is simply living in a fools paradise.

Faithfully yours,

+ William J. Walsh

Archbishop of Dublin.

P.S. I think it a duty to write this, although from information that has just reached me, I am fairly satisfied that the mischief has already been done, and that the country is practically sold.

This letter from the Archbishop of Dublin appeared in the Evening Herald.

Letter from His Grace the Most Rev. Dr. Walsh, Archbishop of Dublin, to His Eminence Cardinal O'Connell of America.

Archbishop's House, Dublin.
10th November, 1919.

My dear Lord Cardinal,

I wish to contribute a hundred guineas (£105 sterling) to the Irish National Fund inaugurated under the auspices of the elected body known as Dáil Éireann, our Irish Parliament. I cannot but think that, as far as our people of Irish race are concerned, their knowledge of the fact that I have subscribed to the Fund would be of as at least as much help as any money subscription of mine could be.

But as matters now stand in Ireland, none of our newspapers dare publish the fact that I have subscribed. We are living under martial law, and amongst the numerous devices to which our present government has had recourse in its foolish attempts to crush the national spirit of our people is the issuing of sundry military orders. In one of these they have given notice to the editors or managers of our popular newspapers to the effect that the fate of any newspaper venturing to publish the names of contributors to the Fund, or the amounts contributed, will be immediate suppression.

Freedom of the Press, the right of public meeting, the right of personal liberty, even the right of trial by jury, no longer exist in this country, except so far as they can exist subject to the absolute uncontrolled discretion of some military ruler technically designated the "competent military authority".

"The competent military authorities" do not seem to realise that there is no possible remedy for this lamentable state of things so long as the source of all evil—the present system of military rule in Ireland—is maintained . . .

William J. Walsh,
Archbishop of Dublin.

SIR JAMES McMAHON'S TRICK

It is the job of civil service chiefs to accomplish in their own secret but audacious and quite ruthless way things which generals and armies could never attempt. That is why "Red Tape" is the cleverest combination of two words ever invented to conceal and cover up 99% of the tracks when 'higher executives' deviate from what the electorate believes it commanded them to do, or not do. For the moment these remarks apply to the head of the Irish Post Office, in Dublin Castle, in 1918, while the General Election campaign was going on. He was James McMahon, one of the few higher civil servants of the period who lived all his life in Ireland; an Armagh born Catholic who ended up as President of the R.D.S.

When he was old, and had grown incautious, and was entertaining Sean T. O'Kelly, then "President of Ireland" during an Aga Khan jumping competition, his mind went back to the early triumph, which put him on the way to the Under Secretaryship, the Privy Council, the confidence of FitzAllen, "First Catholic Viceroy", and the job he brought off in Armagh to cripple Dáil Éireann before it was born. For the moment the two old men are chatting. I quote Sean T.'s account:

"In eight of the Ulster contituencies we had a problem. Our information was that in the majority of these Sinn Fein could win against any Unionist candidate. In a few the Home Rule Party still had a fair following and if the pro-Irish vote were split the Unionist might win. The National Executive nominated Eoin MacNeill and myself to attend a convention . . . to see if we could come to some arrangement. We arranged to allot four of these constituencies to Sinn Fein and four to the Home Rule Party . . . I learned, a few days later, that MacNeill had been persuaded to give the Irish Party one of the seats the convention had allotted to Sinn Fein . . .

"Many years later, I heard from Rt. Hon. James MacMahon how this was brought about . . . He was then the Under Secretary in Dublin Castle—the highest British official in the land . . . While I was President I sat many times beside James MamMahon when he was President of the R.D.S.

"Brought together in this way we often swapped yarns in the President's Box. We talked one day about the 1918 election and he told me that as a close friend of Cardinal Logue, and being in intimate touch with Mr. Joseph Devlin . . . he had been au courant with all that happened at the Dungannon convention . . . the Irish Party felt they should have received six of these seats instead of four. He personally urged that an effort should be made to rectify this position the day of nomination. So he went to Cardinal Logue and got the Cardinal's permission to use his name for this purpose. He rang up Sinn Fein Headquarters and talked to somebody there—he did not remember the name—as the Cardinal's secretary and urged a reconsideration of the convention's decision.

"Anyhow he succeeded in winning an additional seat for the Parliamentary Party, and when talking about it he seemed quite proud of what he had accomplished. He jocularly remarked one day 'you and I could tell many an interesting story about the past fifty years in Ireland. If we collaborated we could write a book'."

The reasons why Sir Edward Carson's party, and the Unionists elected for South County Dublin and Trinity College did not recognise the principle of majority rule in Ireland and boycotted Dáil Éireann at that time, are clear enough. Why did the Catholic Nationalists fail to recognise or attend the Dáil? This is among the major mysteries which can only be uncovered when the papers are released. In Dublin, too, there has been a strange tendency to hold from publication papers, which properly belong to the Nation.

Collins had been released at Christmas, 1916. There was plenty of scope for his great abilities and, unlike Brugha, and Rory O'Connor, he needed a job. A great contribution to his climb to power was made by Tom Cullen (the architect, not to be confused with the other Tom Cullen, of Collins' staff—both fine men!) and Larry Nugent. These two were the officers of a company of National Volunteers who had stayed where they were— probably for reasons of strategy, at the time of the Volunteer split in 1915. They still belonged to the executive of the National Volunteers, and had even received permits from Dublin Castle for acquiring small quantities of arms subsequent to Easter Week. They had done what they could to save arms hidden or discarded after the Rising; above all they had "intelligence" contacts inside Dublin Castle, by means of which they obtained possession of portions of the Castle list of suspects, detached, by accident or otherwise, from the main lists. They turned this material over to Collins—who had emerged from internment at the head of a group of I.R.B. men organised among the prisoners. When Collins was employed as secretary to the National Aid organisation—and presently of the combined Irish Republican Prisoners' Dependants' Fund—he was able to use some of the relief money in weekly payments to unemployed ex-prisoners who were really I.R.B. organisers, cycling through the countryside.

Presently Cullen and Nugent captured the assets of the National Volunteers, including No. 44 Parnell Square, and they provided the political drive which took over some halls and other assets of the A.O.H. (or the Parliamentary Party) when the majority vote veered to Sinn Fein. Their company became "H" Company, 3rd Battalion, Dublin Brigade, I.R.A., and it has been referred to as "headquarters company". Its military record is excellent. Frank Gallagher was a member of this Company. The neighbouring "E" Company was "Dev's Own".—*Larry Nugent's unpublished Memoirs.*

DÁIL ÉIREANN

Alphabetical list of those entitled to sit in Dáil Éireann
R.—Republican; U.—Unionist; N.—Nationalist;
R.-N.—Republican-Nationalist; L.U.-Labour Unionist.

(This list is taken from *Leabhar na hÉireann,* the Irish
Year Book and World Directory, edited by Alasdair
MacCabe, T.D., 1921. There were 105 members, including
4 from the Universities.)

Allen, Col. W. G. (U.) Armagh N.
Anderson, Dr. H. (U.) Derry N.
Archdale, F. M. (U.) Fermanagh N.
Barton, R. C. (R.) Wicklow W.
Beaslai, Piaras (R.) Kerry E.
Blythe, E. (R.) Monaghan N.
Boland, H. (R.) Roscommon S.
Brown, T. W. (U.) Down N.
Buckley, D. (R.) Kildare N.
Burke, J. A. (R.) Tipperary Mid.
Brugha, C. (R.) Waterford Co.
Burn, T. (U.) Belfast, S. Anne's
Carson, Sir E. (U.) Belfast,
　　Duncairn
Clancy, J. J. (R.) Sligo N.
Colivet, P. (R.) Limerick City
Collins, C. (R.) Limerick W.
Collins, M. (R.) Cork S.
Coote, W. (U.) Tyrone S.
Cosgrove, W. P. (R.) Kilkenny N.
Craig, Capt. C. (U.) Antrim S.
Craig, Col. Sir J. (U.) Down Mid.
Crowley, N. J. (R.) Kerry N.
Crowley, D. (R.) Mayo N.
Cusack, Dr. B. (R.) Galway N.
de Valera, Eamon (R.) Mayo E.
de Valera, Eamon (R.) Clare E.
Devlin, J. (N.) Belfast, Falls
Dixon, Capt. H. (U.) Belfast,
　　Pottinger
Dockrell, Sir M. (U.) Dublin
　　Rathmines
Dolan, J. N. (R.) Leitrim
Donald, T. (L.U.) Belfast,
　　Victoria
Donnelly, J. (R.-N.) Armagh, S.
Duffy, Gavan (R.) Dublin, S.
Duggan, E. (R.) Meath, St.
Etchingham, J. (R.) Wicklow E.
Fahy, F. (R.) Galway S.
Fitzgerald, D. (R.) Dublin,
　　Pembroke
Galligan, P. (R.) Cavan W.
Ginnell, L. (R.) Westmeath
Griffith, A. (R.) Cavan East
Griffith, A. (R.) Tyrone N.W.
Harbison, T. (R.-N.) Tyrone N.E.
Hayes, Dr. R. (R.) Limerick E.
Hayes, J. (R.) Cork W.
Henry, D. S. (U.) Derry, S.
Hunter, T. (R.) Cork N.E.

Kelly, F. J. (R.-N.) Donegal E.
Kelly, Ald. T. (R.) Dublin,
　　Stephen's Green
Kent, D. (R.) Cork E.
Kerr-Smiley, Major P. (U.)
　　Antrim N.
Lawless, F. (R.) Dublin Co. N.
Lennon, J. (R.) Carlow
Lindsay, W. A. (U.) Belfast,
　　Cromac.
Lonsdale, J. R. (U.) Armagh Mid.
Lynch, D. (R.) Cork S.E.
Lynch, F. (R.) Kerry S.
Lynn, R. J. (U.) Belfast,
　　Woodvale.
McBride, J. M. (R.) Mayo W.
MacCabe, A. (R.) Sligo S.
McCalmont, Lt.-Col. R. (U.)
　　Antrim E.
McCann, P. (R.) Tipperary E.
　　(dec'd.)
McCartan, Dr. (R.) King's Co.
McDonagh, J. (R.) Tipperary N.
McGrath, J. (R.) Dublin,
　　St. James.
McGuffin, S. (L.U.) Belfast
　　Shankill.
McGuinness, J. (R.) Longford.
MacEntee, S. (R.) Monaghan S.
MacNeill, E. (R.) National Univ.
MacNeill, E. (R.) Derry City.
MacSwiney, T. (R.) Cork Mid.
MacVeigh, J. (R.-N) Down S.
Maloney, P. J. (R.) Tipperary S.
Markievicz, Mme. (R.) Dublin,
　　St. Patrick's.
Mellows, Liam (R.) Galway E.
Mellows, Liam (R.) Meath N.
Moles, T. (U.) Belfast Ormeau
Mulcahy, R. (R.) Dublin C'tarf.
O'Connor, A. (R.) Kildare S.
O'Doherty, J. (R.) Donegal N.
O'Higgins, B. (R.) Clare W.
O'Higgins, K. (R.) Queen's Co.
O'Keeffe, P. (R.) Cork N.
O'Ceallaigh, S. T. (R.) Dublin,
　　College Green.
O'Ceallaigh, S. S. (R.) Louth
O'Mahony, J. (R.) Fermanagh S.
O'Máille, P. (R.) Galway
　　Connemara

O'Mara, J. (R.) Kilkenny S.
O'Neill, Hon. R. W. (U.) Antrim
    Mid.
Plunkett, Count (R.) Rosc'm'n. N.
Redmond, Capt. W. A. (N.)
    Waterford City
Reid, D. D. (U.) Down E.
Roiste, L. de (R.) Cork City.
Ryan, Dr. J. (R.) Wexford S.
Samuels, A. W. (U.) Dublin Univ.
Sears, W. (R.) Mayo S.

Shanahan, P. (R.) Dublin, H'bour.
Staines, M. (R.) D'b'n., S. Michans
Stack, A. (R.) Kerry W.
Sweeney, J. (R.) Donegal W.
Sweetman, R. (R.) Wexford N.
Ward, P. J. (R.) Donegal S.
Walsh, J. J. (R.) Cork City.
Whitla, Sir W. (U.) Belfast Univ.
Wilson, D. M. (U.) Down W.
Woods, Sir Robert (U.) Dublin Univ.

Attendance at the first meeting of Dáil Éireann as given
in *IRIS DÁIL ÉIREANN*—an Cheud Tionol, 21 Ianuar,
1919 : —

Iolscoil na hEireann	Eoin Mac Néill
Co. na Midhe (Theas)	Eamon O Dubhgháin
Ath Cliath (Cluain Tairbhe)	Risteárd O Maolchatha
Ath Cliath (Faithche an Cholaiste)	Seán T. O Ceallaigh
Cuan na Mara	Pádraig O Máille
Cathair Chorcaighe	S. S. Breathnach
Co. Chorcaighe (Theas)	Micheál O Coileain
Co. Chorcaighe (Thiar)	Seán O hAodha
Doire Colmchille	Eoin Mac Néill
Dun na nGall (Thuaid)	Seosamh O Dochartaigh
Dun na nGall (Theas)	Peadar Mac an Bháird
Dun na nGall (Thiar)	Seosamh Mac Suibhne
Co. Ath Cliath (Theas)	S. Gabhán Ui Dhubhthaigh
Roinn an Chuain (Ath Cliath)	Philib O Seaachain
Co. Chiarraidhe (Thoir)	Piaras Beaslai
Co. Chill Dara (Thuaidh)	Domhnall O Buachalla
Co. Phortlairge	Cathal Brugha
Co. Loch Gormain (Thuadh)	Roger Sweetman
Co. Lughmhaighe	An Dr. S. O Riain
Co. Loch Gormain (Theas)	Conchubhar O Coilean
Co. Luimnighe (Thiar)	Seán S. O Ceallaigh
Co. Mhuigheo (Tuaidh)	An Dr. O Crudhlaoich
Co. Ros Comain (Thuaidh)	S. N. Pluincéad (Count)
Co. Ros Comain (Theas)	Enri O Beolain
Co. Tiobraid Arann (Meadh)	Séamus A. De Burca
Co. Tiobraid Arann (Theas)	P. A. O Maoldomhnaigh
Co. Chill Mhantain (Thiar)	R. C. Barton
Co. Laoise	Caoimhghin O hUigin
Ath Cliath (St. Michan's)	Micheal Mac Stáin
Ath Cliath (Faithche Stiophain)	Tomas O Ceallaigh

At the end of this report we find an item which was intended to confuse the enemy:

Corrigenda.

  "San Rolla i n-ionad
     'Micheal O Coileain i lathair' ba cheart
     'Micheal O Coileain as lathair'.
  agus i n-ionad
     'Enri O Beolain i lathair' ba cheart
     'Enri O Beolain as lathair'."

This was printed by "The Wood" in Fleet St. (previously Liberty Press) where the I.R.B. had an office. The last minute change, when the job was running, resulted from an order to change the correct text, supplied by the secretaries to the Dáil, who included Diarmuid Ó hEigeartaigh of the I.R.B. and Army Council).

DECLARATION OF INDEPENDENCE

Whereas the Irish people is by right a free people:
And Whereas for seven hundred years the Irish people has never ceased to repudiate and has repeatedly protested in arms against foreign usurpation:

And Whereas English rule in this country is, and always has been, based upon force and fraud and maintained by military occupation against the declared will of the people:
And Whereas the Irish Republic was proclaimed in Dublin on Easter Monday, 1916, by the Irish Republican Army acting on behalf of the Irish people:

And Whereas the Irish people is resolved to secure and maintain its complete independence in order to promote the common weal, to re-establish justice, to provide for future defence, to insure peace at home and goodwill with all nations and to constitute a national policy based upon the people's will with equal right and equal opportunity for every citizen:

And Whereas at the threshold of a new era in history the Irish electorate has in the General Election of December, 1918, seized the first occasion to declare by an overwhelming majority its firm allegiance to the Irish Republic:
Now, therefore, we, the elected Representatives of the ancient Irish people in National Parliament assembled, do, in the name of the Irish nation, ratify the establishment of the Irish Republic and pledge ourselves and our people to make this declaration effective by every means at our command:

We ordain that the elected Representatives of the Irish people alone have power to make laws binding on the people of Ireland, and that the Irish Parliament is the only Parliament to which that people will give its allegiance: We solemnly declare foreign government in Ireland to be an invasion of our national right which we will never tolerate, and we demand the evacuation of our country by the English Garrison:

We claim for our national independence the recognition and support of every free nation in the world, and we proclaim that independence to be a condition precedent to international peace hereafter:

In the name of the Irish people we humbly commit our destiny to Almighty God who gave our fathers the courage and determination to persevere through long centuries of a ruthless tyranny, and strong in the justice of the cause which they have handed down to us, we ask His divine blessing on this the last stage of the struggle we have pledged ourselves to carry through to Freedom.

An Ceann Comhairle: A Theachtaí na Dála, tuigfidh sibh ó n-a bhfuil dearbhaighthe annso go bhfuilmíd scartha anois le Sasana. Bíodh a fhios san ag an saoghal, agus ag daoine go mbaineann an scéal leo. Pé nídh a thiocfaidh as a bhfuil ráidhte annso—imirt anma nó bás—tá deire le ré na cainnte in Éirinn, agus má's maith é is mithid é—tá deire le ráiméis.

Tá teachtairí ó fhurmhór a bhfuil de náisiúin sa domhan, ag Bhersailles mar seo, agus is é rud a thug ann iad, ar a n-admháil féinidh, ná chum síothcháin do dhéanamh do chiníbh an domhain ionnus ná beadh a thuilleadh gábha le cogadh choidhche arís. Deirimídna leo anois, agus san go dána, má tháid dá ríre, go gcaithfear briseadh do dhéanamh ar an gceangal so idir an dútha so is Sasana. Muna ndéuntar san ní bheidh aon tsíothcháin ann.

Athchuingím orraibh ionntaoibh do bheith agaibh as a chéile. Tá láimh Dé in ár n-obair: is léir san as ar thárla le dhá bhliain anuas. Dhá bhliain is an Cháisc seo d'imthigh tharainn do bunuigheadh Saorstát Éireann. Ní gábha dhúinn anois acht seasamh le chéile, moladh is buidheachas le Dia. Cuirimís le chéile agus ná déineadh éinne sinn do dheighilt, agus ní baoghal dúinn.

Iarraim ar an dTeachta ó Oirthear Chiarraighe cur leis an dtairgsint.

Piaras Béaslaoi (ó Oirthear Chiarraighe): Is mór an onóir damhsa gur iarradh orm cur leis an ndearbhú ar Fhaisnéis Shaorstáit Éireann. Bhí sé d'amhantar agamsa is ag cuid agaibhse a bheith láithreach nuair do bunuigheadh an Saorstát Seachtmhain na Cásca, 1916, agus bhí laochraidhe cródha ann an uair sin—na daoine do rinn gníomh do réir a dtuairme. Ní mhairid na tréinfhir sin indiu: an namhaid do mhairbh iad. Acht na tréinfhir úd b'iad fé ndear sgéal an lae indiu. Acht bíodh gur mór an truagh ná fuilid na laochraidhe sin in ár measc annso is deimhin dúinn go bhfuil spioraid gach n-aon aca annso in ár dteannta ar an nDáil seo, agus le congnamh Dé leanfaimíd an sompla d'fhágadar san in ar gcomhair.

Deireann an Fhaisnéis go gcuirfam chum cinn an Saorstát ar gach slighe atá in ár gcumas. Cialluigheann san gníomh, agus ní bhfaighmíd staonadh ó éingníomhra, is cuma cad is deire dhóibh, príosún nó dortadh fola. Agus tá muinighin ag muinntir na hÉireann asainn-na, agus againn-na asta san. Déanfaidh Dáil Éireann gach éinnídh chum saoirse do bhaint amach agus chum an Fhaisnéis seo do chur chum críche.

An Ceann Comhairle: Iarraim orraibh éirighe in bhur seasamh agus bréithre na móide seo do rádh im' dhiaidh:
"Aontuighmíd an Fhaisnéis Neamhspleádhchuis seo agus cuirmíd sinn féin fá gheasaibh ár ndícheall do dhéanamh chum í chur i bhfeidhm ar gach slighe ar ár gcumas".
Do rinneadh amhlaidh.

MESSAGE TO THE FREE NATIONS OF THE WORLD

To the Nations of the World! Greeting.

The Nation of Ireland having proclaimed her national independence, calls through her elected representatives in Parliament assembled in the Irish Capital on January 21st, 1919, upon every free nation to support the Irish Republic by recognising Ireland's national status and her right to its vindication at the Peace Congress.

Nationally, the race, the language, the customs and traditions of Ireland are radically distinct from the English. Ireland is one of the most ancient nations in Europe, and she has preserved her national integrity, vigorous and intact, through seven centuries of foreign oppression: she has never relinquished her national rights, and throughout the long era of English usurpation she has in every generation defiantly proclaimed her inalienable right of nationhood down to her last glorious resort to arms in 1916.

Internationally, Ireland is the gateway of the Atlantic. Ireland is the last outpost of Europe towards the West: Ireland is the point upon which great trade routes between East and West converge: her independence is demanded by the Freedom of the Seas: her great harbours must be open to all nations instead of being the monopoly of England. To-day these harbours are empty and idle solely because English policy is determined to retain Ireland as a barren bulwark for English aggrandisement, and the unique geographical position of this island, far from being a benefit and safeguard to Europe and America, is subjected to the purposes of England's policy of world domination.

Ireland to-day reasserts her historic nationhood the more confidently before the new world emerging from the War, because she believes in freedom and justice as the fundamental principles of international law, because she believes in a frank co-operation between the peoples for equal rights against the vested privileges of ancient tyrannies, because the permanent peace of Europe can never be secured by perpetuating military dominion for the profit of empire but only by establishing the control of government in every land upon the basis of the free will of a free people, and the existing state of war, between Ireland and England, can never be ended until Ireland is definitely evacuated by the armed forces of England.

For these among other reasons, Ireland—resolutely and irrevocably determined at the dawn of the promised era of self-determination and liberty that she will suffer foreign dominion no longer—calls upon every free nation to uphold her national claim to complete independence as an Irish Republic against the arrogant pretensions of England founded in fraud and sustained only by an overwhelming military occupation, and demands to be confronted publicly with England at the Congress of Nations, in order that the civilised world having judged between English wrong and Irish right may guarantee to Ireland its permanent support for the maintenance of her national independence.

An Ceann Comhairle. Déanfaidh an Teachta ón Ollscoil Náisiúnta is ó Chathair Dhoire Choim Cille san do thairgsint don Dáil.

Eoin Mac Néill, an Teachta ón Ollscoil Náisiúnta is ó Chathair Dhoire Choim Cille: A Chinn Chómhairle is a mhuinntir na Dála, iarraim orraibh glacadh leis an scéal atá againn dá chur ag triall ar Shaornáisiúnaibh an Domhain. Táimíd ag iarraidh ortha cabhrughadh le Saorstát Éireann. Ní h-amhla atáimíd ag iarraidh ortha Saorstát do chur ar bun i nÉirinn—tá sin déanta cheana. Nílimíd ag iarraidh ortha sinn do chur fé éan chomaoin aca: táimíd ag iarraidh ortha iad féin do chur fé chomaoin aca féin. Molaimíd dóibh é sin do dhéanamh ó cheart, agus muna ndéinid siad é cionnus atá a fhios aca ná go dtiocfadh an lá go mbeadh an scéal chomh dona aca féin is mar atá in Éirinn le na céadtha blian. Ar maithe leó féin iseadh atáimíd ag iarraidh ortha seasamh le cúis na hÉireann fé láthair.

Rud eile, nílimíd-na fé chomaoin ag éan náisiún eile. Ar a mhalairt de chuma atá an scéal—is beag náisiún sa domhan ná fuil fé chomaoin againn-na. Ar náisiún is treise ar domhan indiu, an náisiún is mó atá ag treabhadh ar thaobh na saoirse, bíodh go bhfuil an gníomh le déanamh fós aca.

i. Stáiteanna America, muna mbeadh an chabhair do fuaireadar san ó Éirinn insan tseanaimsir ní bheadh saoirse ná ceart aca féin. B'iad muinntir na hÉireann do thug an cabhair sin dóibh nuair a bhíodar go mór ina gábha, agus muna mbeadh congnamh na nGaedhal, is spioraid an chirt do rug Éireannaigh leó anonn go hAmerica, ní thiocfadh le lucht an U.S.A., saoirse do bhaint amach dóibh féin.

Agus maidir le náisiúin eile: is fada do mhuinntir na hÉireann ag tabhairt dóibh an nídh ba luachmhaire aca. Nuair bhí léigheann is creideamh fé bhláth i nÉirinn thug sí léigheann agus creideamh do sna tíribh eile agus gan éan-rud d'éileamh ina n-ionad. Chuir sí fáilte riamh roimh gach stróinséar ó gach aon pháirt den domhan: nuair a thángadar go h-Éirinn thug sí teagasc dóibh, thug sí leabhra dhóibh in aisce, do bhronn sí ortha gach maitheas dá raibh aici. Agus indiu nuair iompuigheann sí chúcha chum iarraidh ortha seasamh leis an gceart ní comaoin atá aice dá eileamh ortha act cothrom na féinne.

Is truagh ná fuil daoine ó gach náisiún díobh annso indiu, mar do b'fhearrde a gcuid eoluis ar an gcás. Dá mbeidís in Éirinn indiu agus arm dfheicsint anso atá níos líonmhaire go mór ná mar a bhí insa tír éin ré le seacht gcéad bliain anuas, ón gcéad lá do tháinig an Sasanach anall. Agus ba chóir a fhios a bheith ag na náisiúin gurab é an fáth go bhfuilid ann, easbaidh úirlise a bheith ar mhuinntir na hÉireann. Muna mbeadh sin, ní sheasochadh an t-arm san aon tseachtmhain amháin.

An Ceann Comhairle: Cuirfidh an Príomh-Theachta ó Chathair Chorcaighe leis an dtairgsin.

Séamus Breathnach: Tá mórtus mór ormsa an chae do bheith agam ar chur leis an dtairgsint seo.

An Ceann Comhairle: An toil leis an nDáil glacadh leis an méid sin? ("Is toil"). Tá sé glacaithe d'aontoil.

DEMOCRATIC PROGRAMME

We declare in the words of the Irish Republican Proclamation the right of the people of Ireland to the ownership of Ireland, and to the unfettered control of Irish destinies to be indefeasible, and in the language of our first President, Pádraig Mac Phiarais, we declare that the Nation's sovereignty extends not only to all men and women of the Nation, but to all its material possessions, the Nation's soil and all its resources, all the wealth and all the wealth-producing processes within the Nation, and with him we reaffirm that all right to private property must be subordinated to the public right and welfare.

We declare that we desire our country to be ruled in accordance with the principles of Liberty, Equality, and Justice for all, which alone can secure permanence of Government in the willing adhesion of the people.

We affirm the duty of every man and woman to give allegiance and service to the Commonwealth, and declare it is the duty of the Nation to assure that every citizen shall have opportunity to spend his or her strength and faculties in the service of the people. In return for willing service, we, in the name of the Republic, declare the right of every citizen to an adequate share of the produce of the Nation's labour.

It shall be the first duty of the Government of the Republic to make provision for the physical, mental and spiritual well-being of the children, to secure that no child shall suffer hunger or cold from lack of food, clothing, or shelter, but that all shall be provided with the means and facilities requisite for their proper education and training as Citizens of a Free and Gaelic Ireland.

The Irish Republic fully realises the necessity of abolishing the present odious, degrading and foreign Poor Law System, substituting therefor a sympathetic native scheme for the care of the Nation's aged and infirm, who shall not be regarded as a burden, but rather entitled to the Nation's gratitude and consideration. Likewise it shall be the duty of the Republic to take such measures as will safeguard the health of the people and ensure the physical as well as the moral well-being of the Nation.

It shall be our duty to promote the development of the Nation's resources, to increase the productivity of its soil, to exploit its mineral deposits, peat bogs, and fisheries, its waterways and harbours, in the interests and for the benefit of the Irish people.

It shall be the duty of the Republic to adopt all measures necessary for the recreation and invigoration of our industries, and to ensure their being developed on the most beneficial and progressive co-operative and industrial lines. With the adoption of an extensive Irish Consular Service, trade with foreign Nations shall be revived on terms of mutual advantage and goodwill, and while undertaking the organisation of the Nation's trade, import and export, it shall be the duty of the Republic to prevent the shipment from Ireland of food and other necessities until the wants of the Irish people are fully satisfied and the future provided for.

It shall also devolve upon the National Government to seek co-operation of the Governments of other countries in determining a standard of Social and Industrial Legislation with a view to a general and lasting improvement in the conditions under which the working classes live and labour.

An Ceann Comhairle: Iarraim ar an dTeacha ó Chluain Tairbh an méid sin do chur i dtairgsin don Dáil.

Risteárd Ó Maolchatha (Cluain Tairbh): A Chinn Chomhairle agus a lucht na Dála, deinimse an clár so a thairgsin díbh agus iarraim oraibh glacadh leis go fonnmhar agus a bhrígh do chur i bhfeidhm go beacht i nbhur ngníomharthaibh agus i nbhur ndlighthibh. Tá ár dtír agus ár muinntir le fada fé dhaorsmacht agus fé cheangal ár námhad. Táimídne indiu ag briseadh na gceangal agus ag cur na smachta ar neamhnídh, acht tá rian na gceangal agus na hannsmachta uirthe. Siad an obair agus an tráchtáil mórchuislí na tíre. Insna cuislibh sin a théidheann fuil na tíre, an fhuil sin a thugann beatha agus sláinte dá corp agus spionadh dá hanam. Táid siad san i leith na brúidthe agus na briste againn de bhárr na hannsmachta. Níl an rith ceart sa bhfuil agus dá bhárr san tá atanna gránda ann annso agus annsúd ar chorp na tíre, insna catharachaibh, insna bailtibh agus fé'n dtuaith féin. Comhartha dhúinne na hatanna san ar ghalar a raghaidh i méid agus a dhéanfaidh, b'fhéidir, ár dtír do mharbhú mara leighstear é. Má tá uainn ár dtír a mhaireachtaint agus bheith beo i dteannta í d'fhuasgailt caithmíd í shlánú. Deinimís é go cruinn agus go h-ealadhnta. Tuigimís go cruinn sa ghnó san cad is í ár dtír—an Éire seo a bhíonn mar thaidhbhreamh agus mar thairngearacht ag an uile dhuine dá clainn ó thús a óige. Tuigimís gur ab í an tír seo í, áluinn mar a dhein Dia í, saidhbhir le saothar a muinntire, geal le na ngáire, aoibhinn le n-a meidhir, naomhtha le n-a gcreideamh agus a ndeagh-mhéinn. Tuigimís gur ab í an mhuinntir seo againn ag maireachtaint go meidhreach agus go síothchánta imeasg an tsaidhbhris a bhronn Dia ortha agus ghá oibriú chun a gcothuighthe í. Agus nuair a chuirfimíd chun an oibriú san do réidhteach agus do riaghlú, deinimís é ar shlighe a chosgfaidh éinne de lucht miosgais agus foghla ar theacht ag guid an tsaidhbhris dóibh féin agus ag bochtanú na ndaoine.

Ní féidir le náisiún bheith saor an fhaid agus tá an chuid is lugha dá mhuintir gan saoirse. Ní féidir le náisiún bheith beo agus 'na bheathaidh an fhaid agus a dhiúltuighthear d'aon chuid des na daoine a gcion ceart féin den mhaoin agus den tsaidhbhreas a bhronn Dia orainn go léir chun sinn a dheunamh beo, agus chun na beatha bhuanú ionainn. Dá bhrigh sin iarraim oraibh glacadh leis ar rún so. Cuirimís a bhfeidhm i nár reachtaibh é, agus bíodh cuimhne againn a n-ár ngníomharthaibh i gcomhnuidhe ar na daoine gur cúram dúinn iad do theagasg agus do chosaint.

Conchubhar Ó Coileáin, An Teachta ó Iarthar Luimnigh: Do léigheadh an clár sa dá theangain agus dá bhrigh sin is beag duine annso ná tuigeann an scéal. Is mór an t-áthas damhsa cur leis an dtairgsin. Badh mhaith liom a chur ar a súilibh do lucht na Dála cad é a ndualgas i dtaobh an chláir seo. Do cuireadh os bhur gcomhair indiu mórán nidhthe, agus isé bhur ndualgas an cúrsa do leanamhaint go dlúth. Agus budh mhaith liom a chur ina luighe ar mhuinntir na tíre gur chóir dóibh cabhrughadh go dian is go dlúth, ionnas go mbeadh ar a gcumas é chur i ngníomh mar ba cheart.

An Ceann Comhairle: Do chualabhair go léir an méid sin. An toil libh glacadh leis an dtairgsin? ("Is toil"). Tá glacaithe leis d'aonghuth.

An Ceann Comhairle. Ní bhacfar le gnáthriaghla na Dála indiu, acht socrófar iad an chéad lá eile.

An Ceann Comhairle: Táimíd chum na hoibre do chur ar athló go dtí leathuair tar éis a trí amáireach, acht beidh cruinniughadh príobháideach againn annsoin.

Eóin Mac Néill (ón Ollscoil Náisiúnta, is ó Chathair Dhoire Cholmchille): Cuirimse leis an dtairgsint sin. (Do glacadh leis d'aonghuth.)

D'éirigh An Dáil as an dtionól ar a 5.20 iar nóin.

SOURCES

Thom's Directory.
Irish Times "Sinn Fein Rebellion Handbook".
"Ireland Dupe or Heroine", the Earl of Midleton, K.P.
"The Irish Volunteers", Rev. Prof. Martin.
"The Neutrality of Ireland", Henry Harrison.
Col. Maurice Moore's paper in N. Library.
Dáil Reports.
Unpublished statements—Anna Parnell, Helena Molony, Larry Nugent.
"James O'Mara", Patricia Lavelle.
"Arthur Griffith", Padraig Colum.
"Allegiance", Robert Brennan.
"The Irish Republic", Dorothy Macardle.
Thomas Davis Lectures.
Irish Labour Party and T.U.C. reports.
Sir James O'Connor.
"Limerick's Fighting Story", Kerryman.

"Irish Citizen Army", Fox.
American Commission on Conditions in Ireland.
Cumann Leigheacht an Phobal.
"Red Terror and Green", Richard Dawson. 1920.
"Michael Collins", Beaslai. 1926.
Political writings of P. H. Pearse and James Connolly.
Desmond Greaves' "Life of James Connolly".
Labour in Irish History.
Labour, Nationality and Religion.
With De Valera in America, Dr. P. McCartan.
Leabhar na hÉireann, the Irish Year Book, 1921, Alasdair MacCabe, T.D.
Dáil official report of first day's proceedings, Liberty Press, 1919.
The Issue, Sinn Fein pamphlet.
History of England, A. J. P. Taylor.
Politics in Wartime, A. J. P. Taylor, Hamish Hamilton.
A Short History of the World, H. G. Wells, The Bodley Head.
Life of Michael Davitt, Cashman.
The Life and Times of James Connolly, Desmond C. Greaves.
Life of Lord Carson, Colvin.
Between Capitalism and Socialism, Rev. P. Coffey, Ph.D., Maynooth.
Chronology, Buro Staire Mileatha.
Fr. Michael O'Flanagan, C. Desmond Greaves.
Markievicz papers, Mrs. M. McMahon.
Moynihan papers.
Mr. Joseph Cashman's photographs.
Irish Press.
Irish Independent, Evening Herald.
Belfast Newsletter.
Handbook of the Ulster Question.
Voice of Ireland, William G. Fitzgerald, courtesy Miss McCauley.
T.U.C. reports loaned by Michael McInerney and Donal Nevin.